Feminist Film Theory and *Pretty Woman*

FILM THEORY IN PRACTICE

Series Editor: Todd McGowan

Editorial Board

Slavoj Žižek, University of Ljubljana, Slovenia
Joan Copjec, Brown University, USA
Hilary Neroni, University of Vermont, USA
Jennifer Friedlander, Pomona College, USA
Fabio Vighi, University of Cardiff, UK
Hugh Manon, Clark University, USA
Paul Eisenstein, Otterbein University, USA
Hyon Joo Yoo, University of Vermont, USA
Louis-Paul Willis, University of Quebec, Canada

FILM THEORY IN PRACTICE

Feminist Film Theory and *Pretty Woman*

MARI RUTI

Bloomsbury Academic
An imprint of Bloomsbury Publishing Inc

BLOOMSBURY
NEW YORK · LONDON · OXFORD · NEW DELHI · SYDNEY

Bloomsbury Academic
An imprint of Bloomsbury Publishing Plc

1385 Broadway	50 Bedford Square
New York	London
NY 10018	WC1B 3DP
USA	UK

www.bloomsbury.com

BLOOMSBURY and the Diana logo are trademarks of Bloomsbury Publishing Plc

First published 2016

© Mari Ruti, 2016

All rights reserved. No part of this publication may be reproduced or transmitted in any form or by any means, electronic or mechanical, including photocopying, recording, or any information storage or retrieval system, without prior permission in writing from the publishers.

No responsibility for loss caused to any individual or organization acting on or refraining from action as a result of the material in this publication can be accepted by Bloomsbury or the author.

Library of Congress Cataloging-in-Publication Data
A catalog record for this book is available from the Library of Congress.

ISBN: HB: 978-1-5013-1942-6
PB: 978-1-5013-1946-4
ePUB: 978-1-5013-1943-3
ePDF: 978-1-5013-1944-0

Series: Film Theory in Practice

Cover design: Alice Marwick
Cover images: Top image © CSA-Archive / Getty Images Bottom image: Pretty Woman (1990) © Touchstone Pictures / The Kobal Collection

Typeset by Deanta Global Publishing Services, Chennai, India

To Ritva Ruti, a pretty woman if ever there was one.

CONTENTS

Acknowledgments viii

   Introduction 1
1 Feminist Film Theory 17
2 Feminist Film Theory and *Pretty Woman* 101
   Conclusion 177

Notes 183
Further Reading 195
Index 197

ACKNOWLEDGMENTS

Writing a book on *Pretty Woman* for Todd McGowan's film theory series is the most insane intellectual endeavor I've ever undertaken. Although I thank Todd for pushing me to embrace the task, I'm not sure I'll ever recover from the sheer terror of it. My research assistant Julia Cooper deserves my gratitude for having been my reliable go-to girl on countless bits of movie trivia. Finally, I thank my mother, to whom this book is dedicated, for having taught me the rudiments of fashion when I was too young to protest. Without this early education, this book would surely not exist.

Introduction

When the television show *Alias* (2001–06)—starring Jennifer Garner as the tough and toned CIA undercover agent Sydney Bristow—introduces Bradley Cooper as Sydney's friend, Will, we find out that he has had a dreadful blind date. When Sydney asks him what went wrong, Will snidely responds, "Her favorite movie of all time. You ready for this? *Pretty Woman*." This scene, which takes place in the pilot episode, is important for establishing Sydney's credibility as a CIA agent: Will's disparaging tone implies that only silly women watch movies like *Pretty Woman* (1990) whereas smart, strong, and resourceful women like Sydney would never waste their time on such mindless fluff.

Although I'm partial to Sydney's version of ass-kicking womanhood, it seems worth considering the implications of Will's easy dismissal of *Pretty Woman*: a movie that has retained a massive female following during the quarter of a century since its release. Back in 1990 *Pretty Woman*—directed by Garry Marshall—surprised Hollywood and movie critics alike by becoming the year's second most popular movie. At the time, it was unusual for movies aimed at female audiences to climb to the top of the box office charts. Nor was Julia Roberts yet a star. Her role in *Mystic Pizza* (1988) had brought her some attention. But it was her *Pretty Woman* role as the spirited prostitute, Vivian Ward, who captures the heart of the cynical corporate raider Edward Lewis (Richard Gere), that made her Hollywood royalty.

By now *Pretty Woman* has attained an iconic status within our cultural imagination in the sense that even people who haven't seen the movie tend to know something about it.

At the same time, Will's mocking assessment of the movie is by no means unusual: if his disdainful view of women who like *Pretty Woman* works so well to mark, by contrast, Sydney as a woman to be reckoned with, it's because it's instantly comprehensible; it's a form of cultural shorthand regarding the frivolity of romantic comedies and the shallowness of the women who watch them. And who is going to argue with it, particularly if the lens one is going to apply to the movie is that of feminist film theory, as I do in this book?

I'm not going to argue that *Pretty Woman* is the best movie of all time. But I want to begin by pointing out that there is something questionable about our society's routine disparagement of romantic comedies—a genre affiliated with women and femininity specifically. As I'll show in the second half of this book, *Pretty Woman* was attacked vehemently by both mainstream and academic critics in the years after its release. The same fate has met so many other popular romantic comedies that one has to wonder whether it's actually true that these movies are intrinsically (and consistently) awful or whether critics are predisposed to deem any movie that falls within the romcom category—that is, any movie that explicitly targets female viewers—awful.

It's telling that critics who lauded the 2011 smash hit *Bridesmaids* often praised it for not being a "typical" romcom. *Bridesmaids* was widely depicted as a chick flick that (surprisingly) doesn't suck. As one critic helpfully put it, "Don't worry: it's not *Sex and the City*."[1] Such reassurances made *Bridesmaids* a movie that even *men* might find worth watching. As Joe Morgenstern of *The Wall Street Journal* announced with a degree of bravado, "If this is only a chick flick, then call me a chick."[2] *Only a chick flick?* Morgenstern's wording suggests that a movie that *only* appeals to women is inherently worthless. In other words, his enthusiasm for *Bridesmaids* rests on an everyday misogyny that he doesn't even see the need to hide, presumably because he knows that he's uttering a taken-for-granted assessment of both romcoms and the "chicks" who watch them.

Equally interesting are the reasons that raised *Bridesmaids* from the romcom ghetto to a movie worth seeing: crass language, explicit sex, and an extended gross-out scene during which women vomit all over each other, Maya Rudolph defecates on the street, and Melissa McCarthy, well, shits in a sink. As the *New York Times* sums up the matter, *Bridesmaids* "goes where no typical chick flick does: the gutter."[3] In the words of Frank Kermore of the *Observer*, in turn, *Bridesmaids* is a "*ballsy* comic hit."[4] It therefore seems that the best way for a romcom to gain critical acclaim is to become a female version of *The Hangover* (2009).

Don't get me wrong. I like *Bridesmaids*. I'm not saying that the movie didn't deserve the praise it received. Moreover, from a feminist perspective, it's not clear which is worse: critics implying that *Bridesmaids* is a great movie because it's too ballsy to be a typical chick flick or critics implying that its "ballsiness" goes too far because—in the words of Peter Travers of *Rolling Stone*—"guys and gross make a better fit."[5] Travers suggests that there is something wrong ("unnatural" even) about women running wild. I can't endorse this view. The point I'm making is merely that it's worth contemplating the fact that our culture—mainstream movie critics, many film scholars within the academy, and the average guy on the street alike—tends to more or less automatically belittle romantic comedies even though (or perhaps *because*?) the genre values love, emotions, relationships, and female friendships over violence and vomiting.

Diane Negra notes that "mainstream cinematic romances are customarily held in low cultural esteem and their review discourses often reflect the low expectations attached to them."[6] Along related lines, Tamar Jeffers McDonald remarks that romcoms "are viewed as 'guilty pleasures' which should be below one's notice."[7] Helen Warner in turn observes that romcoms have "struggled to gain the cultural legitimacy accorded to many other ('masculine') Hollywood genres."[8] Such trivialization of romcoms is far from neutral but reveals a great deal about our society's gender politics: movies that place a female character—often a notably feisty one—at the center of a story that showcases her wittiness and competence are rated lower than movies where men can't remember where they parked their car (as in the 2000 *Dude, Where's My Car?*).

It's of course true that romcoms offer us impossibly attractive heroines, depoliticized plots, and makeover scenes designed to warm the calculating hearts of capitalist entrepreneurs. I'm not saying that there aren't things to criticize in these movies. As we'll see in the course of this book, much about them merits critical scrutiny. But the commonly accepted notion that in comparison with "real" movies, movies like *Pretty Woman* represent sentimental drivel seems akin to the idea—once also commonly accepted—that in comparison with "real" literature, Jane Austen's *Pride and Prejudice* (1813) is limited to trifling "feminine" concerns.

But isn't the point of romantic comedies to usher the heroine, however witty and competent, into the protective arms of a knight in shining armor? And doesn't *Pretty Woman* in particular offer a heinously retrograde vision of gender relations? How could a feminist critic such as myself find anything redeeming in a movie like this? These are fair questions that I hope to address in the pages to come. At this point, let me simply say that I'm less interested in labeling *Pretty Woman* as either retrograde or progressive than I am in understanding why so many women—including those with explicitly feminist sensibilities—find it so riveting.

I've already noted the movie's box office success. Furthermore, *Pretty Woman* has over the years remained one of the most rewatched movies in Hollywood's history, offering for many viewers what Hilary Radner describes as a "satisfying and uplifting effect."[9] Even women who were toddlers—and sometimes not even born—when the movie was released frequently admit liking it. It's then not surprising that the movie has become a template for countless other romcoms to imitate. The success of *When Harry Met Sally* (1989)—released a year before *Pretty Woman*—had already intimated a shift in Hollywood. But it was *Pretty Woman* that launched a new Hollywood era: the era of the contemporary romantic comedy.

Radner characterizes *Pretty Woman* as "a neo-romantic comedy."[10] In a way, the movie signaled the return of a genre that had remained largely dormant since the lively romantic (often screwball) comedies of the 1930s and 1940s. The latter—movies such as *Forsaking All Others* (1934), *Bringing Up Baby* (1938), *His Girl Friday* (1940), *The Philadelphia Story* (1940), *The Bride Came C.O.D.* (1941), *She Wouldn't Say Yes* (1945), and *Adam's Rib* (1949), among many others—showcased strong heroines such as Joan Crawford, Bette Davis, Katharine Hepburn, and Rosalind Russell. These heroines were frequently opinionated, resourceful, and career oriented. In addition, they were unquestionably the center of the filmic universe they inhabited: the spotlight was clearly on these spunky women. Equally importantly, the male leads (think of Cary Grant and Spencer Tracy) of these films tended to be polite, polished, and gentlemanly. Even when—as was often the case—the dialogue between the male and female leads consisted of animated sparring, the men eventually turned out to be genteel, even aristocratic, thereby offering appealing screen idols for female spectators.

This world of bold women and gentle men—a world that, moreover, privileged the point of view of the female lead—is what *Pretty Woman* and subsequent romantic comedies have attempted to resurrect. Radner is right to argue that, due to its immense success, *Pretty Woman* defined "the lineaments of the new girly film that successive examples of the genre would progressively elaborate."[11] As Radner's wording implies, the heroines of today's romantic comedies tend to be more "girly" than the heroines of their 1930s and 1940s counterparts (a theme I'll explore extensively). But what interests us at the moment is that there is also a great deal of continuity between the 1930s and 1940s heroines played by, say, Katharine Hepburn and Julia Roberts's Vivian: these women are funny, capable, confident, and not easily pushed around by the men in their lives.

Here is my first tentative response to the questions I raised above about the retrograde elements of romantic comedies: romcoms are rarely completely backward. Like their 1930s and 1940s predecessors, they defy straightforward categorization as either antifeminist or feminist, for they tend to present an ambiguous mixture of conservative and empowering elements.[12] For instance, while *Pretty Woman*'s romance plot remains traditional, Vivian is portrayed as independent, outspoken, sexually assertive, and openly defiant of dominant social conventions. Such a jumble of antifeminist and feminist ingredients makes it a perplexing site of study.

This may explain why female students who enroll in my undergraduate courses on feminist film theory often seem to do so in the hope of putting an end to their ambivalence toward movies such as *Pretty Woman*. *Why can't I stop watching these movies?* is a question students frequently pose at the beginning of the semester, sometimes with a degree of self-flagellation, as if liking romcoms were a breach of their feminist politics. By the end of the semester they come to see that if they're confused, it's not because they aren't able to think clearly, let alone because they're bad feminists, but because romcoms offer an inherently confusing terrain of gender and sexuality.

The confusion of my students reflects a more general confusion in our society. In recent years, feminist film theorists—like feminist theorists generally speaking—have struggled to grasp the ambiguous ways in which feminism is both rejected by and incorporated into contemporary culture, which some characterize as postfeminist, others as neofeminist, and yet others as antifeminist. I'll outline some of this complexity in the first half of this book. Here I merely want to note that one of the main characteristics of this ambiguous cultural landscape—which gained momentum during the 1990s, the very decade that *Pretty Woman* helped usher into existence—is that it wants to retain many of the victories of second-wave feminism (the feminism of the 1960s and 1970s) while simultaneously proclaiming feminism dead;

it wants to transcend, and frequently even ridicules, the very political movement—feminism—to which women owe the freedoms that allow them to declare feminism unnecessary. In a way, it wants to assert that *of course* men and women are now equal but that this has nothing to do with feminism, which is reckoned to be boring, outdated, aggrieved, and—by a curious twist of logic—sometimes even bad for women.

Recently pop stars such as Beyoncé and Taylor Swift have started to reverse this negative perception of feminism by taking an interest in it. But since the 1990s, feminism has been a dirty word among many young women. Academic feminists who possess a historical understanding of the cultural forces that have led to this vilification of feminism sometimes find this situation frustrating, not the least because they realize that the way they define feminism is quite different from how nonacademic women who reject it understand it.

While the word "on the street" seems to be that feminists are man-hating, sex-hating, and fun-hating destroyers of pleasure, many academic feminists are interested in enriching the lives of both men and women by freeing them from the coercive definitions of acceptable masculinity and femininity that our culture has traditionally imposed on them. Many third-wave (post-1990) feminists believe that besides the equality of men and women, the goal of feminism is to deconstruct the binaristic models of gender that govern our society so as to open up a greater array of human possibility for all genders: cis-men, cis-women, and genderqueers of any sexual orientation,[13] transgendered people, and other modalities of gendered expression.

According to this definition of feminism, the system of male domination—patriarchy—must be dissociated from individual men, many of whom find this system just as unpalatable as feminists do (and some of whom even identify as feminists, as some of my male colleagues and students do). As a result, contemporary feminists usually don't see men, or at least not all of them, as the enemy of women but rather as fellow travelers toward more satisfying modes of dwelling in the world. The aim of such feminism is not to fan the battle of the sexes but to work together with enlightened men to create ways of life that feel more rewarding to everyone. Such feminism is usually also emphatically sex-positive: far from rejecting sexuality, it wants better sex for all of those who find sex interesting.

Third-wave feminism also shies away from a single-minded focus on gender inequality as the only source of evil. Instead, it interrogates the manner in which various axes of social oppression—having to do with race, class, religion, gender, and sexual orientation, among other factors—intersect to produce a social fabric where some people have unfair advantages whereas others suffer from unfair discrimination. Essentially, it attempts to understand how impersonal, structural forces of inequality allow some people to thrive while keeping others down so that—contrary to what our society's dominant ideology tells us—individual effort alone is not always enough to ensure success, happiness, or the so-called good life.

Perhaps this is one reason that so many young women resent feminism. Perhaps they don't want to hear that there are any structural impediments to their success, wanting to believe, instead, that if they just try hard enough, their lives will turn out beautifully. This is the American dream, isn't it? Unfortunately, for many individuals, it's destined to remain just that: a dream.

Beyond this stumbling block, women who reject feminism—who view themselves as postfeminist—often do so because they believe that feminism is incompatible with femininity. As I'll demonstrate in this book, the main bone of contention between second-wave feminists and the younger generation of postfeminist women that emerged in the 1990s was about how femininity should be understood. Second-wave feminists tended to be critical of traditional incarnations of femininity because they recognized that these incarnations had throughout the centuries been used to label women as inferior creatures unfit for social, political, and economic equality. Young postfeminist women, in contrast, wanted—and still do—their lipstick, nail polish, miniskirts, high heels, and push-up bras.

It's unfortunate that postfeminist women didn't realize that by the 1990s, (third-wave) feminism had come to the same conclusion: though I wouldn't go as far as to claim that push-up bras were a major concern for third-wave feminism, one of its defining features was—and continues to be—that it doesn't view feminism and femininity as antithetical to each other. If anything, it recognizes that the (often implicit) denigration of femininity that *some*—but by no means all—second-wave feminists engaged in could be viewed as a form of sexism (and, incidentally, not unrelated to the cultural condemnation of romcoms I've outlined).

By 2015, when I'm writing this book, third-wave feminism is being superseded by what some call "fourth-wave" feminism and others refuse to slot into the "wave" model altogether.[14] The outlines of this emerging feminism remain somewhat nebulous but the renunciation of femininity doesn't seem to be a part of it. In other words, the assumption that feminism and femininity are mutually exclusive is relatively alien to many academic feminists, such as myself. This explains why it's sometimes hard for me to understand what postfeminist women are attacking when they rail against feminism: what they call "feminism" is an entity I don't recognize even though I've taught feminist theory for more than two decades.

This is not to say that contemporary feminists have abandoned the main ideals of second-wave feminists, for they still see the social parity of the genders as an important goal, criticize media portrayals of hypersexualized femininity, demand equal pay for equal work, and complain about the double burden of professional and domestic work that many women can't seem to escape. But what has changed is precisely the attitude toward femininity. By this I don't mean that contemporary feminists accept any and all representations of femininity, that they're always sympathetic to the uncritical revival of conventional tropes of femininity that characterizes our current cultural environment. We'll discover that many of them view this revival as a clever ruse of heteropatriarchy, as a means of turning women's subordination into something that women "choose" to relish because it comes packaged in the shiny wrapping paper of Victoria's Secret, Christian Louboutin, Dolce & Gabbana, and Louis Vuitton. Still, contemporary feminists are less likely to disparage femininity than many postfeminist women appear to assume.

You can already see why things are so muddled: contemporary feminism isn't necessarily irreconcilable with all aspects of "feminine" culture yet postfeminism—which in some instances functions as an explicit backlash against feminism—routinely broadcasts that it is, with the result that many young women recoil from feminism. Yet if we stick to the most rudimentary definition of feminism—namely that it aspires to guarantee the social, political, and economic equality of men and women—we must admit that there is something bizarre about this recoil, for it implies that women think that men should be socially, politically, and economically superior to them. I doubt that this is what they actually think. Consequently, it seems important to try to understand how it came about that so many young women chose to discard the idea that they need a political movement that protects their equality.

I'll tell some of this story in Chapter 1. But I'll say right away that at its core resides the rise of what social critics call *neoliberalism*: a culture that idealizes individual effort, high productivity, good performance, constant self-improvement, and merit-based achievement. This culture also emphasizes the pleasures of consumerism. The late twentieth century—which in the United States witnesses the Reagan-Bush era of conspicuous consumption—is when neoliberalism crystallized as a creed that promotes the link between personal effort and eventual success, including the ability to spend money. Though the American dream had long preached the notion that striving will be rewarded, neoliberalism amplified this message, promising that individual exertion would result in the good life: a life of self-actualization, professional acclaim, romantic fulfillment, harmonious families, and consumerist fantasies come true.

As this book will illustrate, romcoms like *Pretty Woman* were instrumental in disseminating this ideology, distinctive for its strongly individualistic tone, among a new generation of women who were already turning away from feminism as a seemingly obsolete political movement. Romcoms offer the seductive role model of a female go-getter who—through her intellect, abilities, and ambition—manages to attain both personal and romantic fulfillment. In this sense, they're not exactly antifeminist even if they're not entirely feminist either. At the same time, they tend to celebrate consumerism—including the mentality of shop till you drop—in ways that are difficult to reconcile even with forms of feminism that are otherwise friendly to femininity. Simply put, romcoms routinely suggest that it's through the meticulous cultivation of a commercially constructed femininity—of a "look" that costs a bundle of money—that women are able to attain the life that they've always wanted. You can see how feminism came to lose some of its luster during the 1990s revival of the romantic comedy: Who needs feminism when a trip to Rodeo Drive will do the trick?

This shift from (politicized) feminism to a (depoliticized) "feminine" ethos of consumerism characterizes postfeminist culture, generally speaking. This is one of the many ways in which postfeminism is compatible with neoliberalism. As the second half of Chapter 1 will demonstrate, it's difficult to think about one without the other. Most importantly for our purposes, we'll discover that the harmonious blending of postfeminism and neoliberalism resulted in a significant change in women's attitudes toward their sexual objectification.

During the height of second-wave feminism, many women saw female sexual objectification as a major problem: they found it demeaning that women's worth was being assessed primarily on the basis of their appearance and sexual desirability. This is one reason that female sexual objectification was a central concern for feminist film theory of the 1970s and 1980s, when the field was finding its sea legs. As we'll learn shortly, many prominent feminist film critics of this era were preoccupied with what came to be known as "the male gaze": the manner in which mainstream movies turn women into eroticized objects for men to look at, admire, and—in some instances—critically assess.

Some people in today's culture are still bothered by female sexual objectification. But one of the most noticeable trends of postfeminist society is that many straight women seem to actively welcome their own objectification. Trying to look "hot" in order to elicit men's admiration is no longer disparaged as an antifeminist practice but is seen as the epitome of female empowerment. What could be more enabling than yoking men to their crotches? A cynical reading of the situation might assert that the omnipresence of online pornography has forced women to compete with porn images in order to activate male desire. I'll return to this possibility at the end of Chapter 1. But other cultural forces, such as romcoms that valorize the myriad ways in which women are empowered by enhancing their sex appeal, have played an important role as well.

Consider the makeover scenes that are a stock component of romantic comedies. Their purpose is almost always to establish the female protagonist as an object of desire for her love interest. Yet they invariably *also* signal the beginning of the heroine's ascent from her underdog status to whatever triumph—and there must always be a triumph of some kind—she's destined for. In *Pretty Woman*, it's Julia Roberts's makeover that allows her to marry a billionaire; in *Miss Congeniality* (2000), it's Sandra Bullock's makeover that allows her to solve her FBI case; in *The Princess Diaries* (2001), it's Anne Hathaway's makeover that allows her to become a princess; in *Maid in Manhattan* (2002), it's Jennifer Lopez's makeover that allows her to rise from a hotel maid to the manager of the same hotel. In all of these instances—and in many others—the heroine's makeover is rewarded both by romantic fulfillment and by an increase in personal (and frequently even professional) empowerment. One can see how the insistent repetition of this fantasy inspires the notion that sexual self-objectification is women's fastest route to success; it explains why some of my students proclaim Beyoncé to be the most powerful woman on earth not because she's a talented artist but because she's willing to display vast acreages of skin in her music videos.

In this context, it's important to stress that the cultural shift I've depicted—the shift from condemning female sexual objectification to actively delighting in it—is less about the experience of pleasure than about how this pleasure is interpreted. Feminist film critics knew back in the 1970s and 1980s that many female spectators enjoyed watching women's sexual objectification on screen. The difference is that this enjoyment bothered not just these critics but also many of the spectators themselves, so that one of the main questions of early feminist film theory was, precisely, why women seemed to take pleasure in their own objectification even when they, rationally, believed that they shouldn't.

As my earlier anecdote about female students who enroll in my film theory courses reveals, some women still feel torn by this predicament. But they appear to be in the minority in the sense that many of today's straight women seem to accept their pleasure in their own objectification relatively straightforwardly, without much guilt or agony. That women are sexually objectified in our society seems to be just the way "things are," a commonplace that it seems pointless to resist. And aren't men also objectified—so what's the problem?

This is yet another question I'll take up in Chapter 1. More generally, the first half of this book outlines some of the main concerns of feminist film theory since its inception in the 1970s until the present day. We'll see that the field can—broadly speaking—be divided into two fairly distinctive eras. The first, spanning the 1970s and 1980s, borrowed heavily from the (then) burgeoning fields of psychoanalysis and poststructuralism to develop sophisticated vocabularies for investigating issues such as the social (and filmic) construction of masculinity and femininity, the masquerade of femininity, the male gaze, voyeurism, fetishism, female spectatorship, and cinematic suture (the process by which spectators are sewn into the movie narrative). The second (current) era hasn't lost track of these themes but it tends to focus more strongly on twenty-first-century concerns about neoliberalism, postfeminism, consumerism, female self-objectification, and the resurgence of "girliness" as a new feminine ideal both in mainstream movies and in our culture at large. Both approaches are relevant to the analysis of *Pretty Woman*, the task I'll undertake in Chapter 2.

One of the noteworthy things about *Pretty Woman* is its status as a movie that was released at the threshold of the "watershed" decade of the 1990s, the decade that separates early forms of feminist film theory from its contemporary forms. In retrospect, it's obvious that the movie already foregrounded themes that have since the turn of the twenty-first century become central to feminist media studies. But it took some time for the academy to catch up with the cultural transformations reflected in the movie. As I've already started to suggest, it's precisely the 1990s that witnessed the rise of the "girly film," the type of film that celebrates the construction of femininity as a specifically commercial product. *Pretty Woman*—with its extended makeover and shopping scenes—in many ways pioneered this genre.

Pretty Woman also pioneered the mixture of traditional romance, (neoliberal) postfeminism, and popular feminism that became the trademark of romcoms to come. It's the persistence of traces of feminism that perhaps most interests us. Susan Douglas has coined a term for this: "embedded feminism."[15] Embedded feminism refers to seemingly nonfeminist contexts that take a number of second-wave feminist principles for granted. We'll learn that *Pretty Woman* contains a higher than expected level of such embedded feminism. Among other things, it works overtime to ensure that its fairytale love plot doesn't offend female spectators who are looking for images of female autonomy and competence.

As I've already noted, what makes *Pretty Woman*—like later romantic comedies—a surprisingly complex object of study is that it walks a tightrope between retrograde, potentially antifeminist themes and progressive, potentially feminist ones. These retrograde and progressive themes slide around unpredictably, compete with each other, and generate a veritable mess of conflicting messages about gender and sexuality. My goal is to chart a path through this mess not only to elucidate the pleasure that female audiences have over the years taken in this film but also to assess the relatively serious questions it—like many other romantic comedies—raises about female identity, worth, desire, and the struggle to reconcile the demands of gender equality with the enticements of femininity.

This book starts with an outline of the major concepts and concerns of feminist film theory. However, I don't attempt to provide an exhaustive summary. Rather, I accentuate themes that are most relevant to the study of mainstream Hollywood movies, particularly romantic comedies. This is to say that the choices I made regarding the aspects of feminist film theory that I wanted to highlight in Chapter 1 were guided by my knowledge that I was going to need a specific set of tools for my analysis of *Pretty Woman* in Chapter 2.

This doesn't mean that there is a seamless correspondence between the materials of the two chapters, that I use every bit of theory explained in Chapter 1 in the interpretation of Chapter 2. Some parts of Chapter 1 are designed to offer general background to feminist film theory. But the centrality of *Pretty Woman* to this book caused me to leave out elements of feminist film theory—particularly those related to avant-garde and other alternative films—that might otherwise be included in an overview of the field. The centrality of *Pretty Woman*—and, more generally, of the genre of romantic comedies—to this book also explains its heterosexual slant. I can only apologize to my queer readers by mentioning that queer theory is a topic I address in detail elsewhere.[16]

This book's focus on a mainstream Hollywood movie also accounts for the importance of the following questions to my inquiry: What makes Hollywood film such a powerful component of American—and increasingly global—culture? What is it about the techniques and main tropes of this medium that audiences find so compelling? Additionally, what does

Hollywood film—explicitly or implicitly—teach us about how we're supposed to live, what happiness consists of, and how relationships function (or should function)? Does it serve as an insidious form of ideological (neoliberal) control? Or does it contain progressive elements that push our culture to become less constrictive (e.g., more tolerant of the fluidities of gender and sexuality)? It seems obvious that Hollywood movies are an influential site for the fashioning of desire, fantasy, pleasure, and our visions of the good life. What remains to be determined is the degree to which they can function as advocates for the kind of social change that women—and even feminists—might be able to celebrate.

CHAPTER ONE

Feminist Film Theory

Feminist film theory—like other academic feminist endeavors, such as feminist literary criticism—emerged from the political upheavals of the 1960s. Second-wave feminism had taught women to read their cultural environment critically so as to better understand their socially, politically, and economically subordinate status. It therefore made sense that the critics who developed the field of feminist film studies in the 1970s initially focused primarily on how women were represented—or misrepresented—in Hollywood film and other mass media; it made sense that they took a strong interest in the negative images of women propagated by mainstream culture.

Such early criticism assumed a relatively straightforward relationship between reality and representation, frequently calling for more "realistic" images of women in movies. The methodology used was loosely sociological: a survey of the various ways in which women were stereotyped on screen. More specifically, early feminist film critics asserted that the limited array of female characters (sex object, brainless bimbo, femme fatale, housewife, sacrificing mother, and so on) found in film curtailed women's real-life aspirations, channeling them into an equally limited array of life paths. Furthermore, early feminist film critics were convinced that the incessant repetition of negative female stereotypes bolstered the prejudices of male viewers, thereby strengthening the patriarchal status quo. A well-known example of this early feminist approach is Molly

Haskell's *From Reverence to Rape* (1974), which opens with the following claim: "The big lie perpetrated on Western society is the idea of women's inferiority," and the movie business is "an industry dedicated for the most part to reinforcing the lie."[1]

By the mid-1970s, the sociological approach to feminist film criticism found a rival in a more explicitly theoretical approach, which drew heavily on psychoanalysis and other newly fashionable critical vocabularies, such as French poststructuralism. Because this rival approach provided more sophisticated interpretative strategies, it quickly overtook—though it never entirely silenced—the sociological strand of film criticism, and it's what I'll focus on in the first half of this chapter. However, before we leave behind the sociological approach, I want to stress that it served as an important antecedent to a style of feminist media criticism that has gained prominence in the twenty-first century, often under the auspices of what is called "cultural studies." This style of criticism will be the topic of the second half of this chapter.

One reason that twenty-first-century feminist media criticism contains clear echoes of the early sociological approach is that the latter already foregrounded a theme that remains pressing for many contemporary feminist critics, namely that there is an obvious connection between women's experiences of sexual objectification in the "real" world and their sexual objectification on screen. It's virtually impossible to be a woman in today's (Western) society without understanding that the random guy on the street who tells you that you have a nice ass and the images that flit across the various screens—television, computer, billboard, and movie screens—that populate our lives are part and parcel of the same cultural mentality: a mentality that insists that straight women are passive objects of desire whereas straight men get to be its active subjects.

We'll see below that it's actually psychoanalytic feminist film theory that offered the most powerful articulation of this insight. But early sociological criticism already recognized its significance. And contemporary cultural approaches continue to fixate on it. The basic idea is as simple as it is exasperating: in our heteropatriarchal society, men get to decide what (or whom) they want whereas women's wants are secondary in the sense that their task is merely to turn themselves into enticing objects for male desire. According to this line of reasoning, men actively "own" their desire whereas women's desire is limited to the (passive) desire *to be desired*.

This formulation has been challenged in various ways during the last few decades—and we'll in due course find our way to the objections—but on an elementary level its explanatory power seems so indisputable that it persistently finds its way to feminist film criticism. If anything, some of the objections have recently fallen to the wayside as a result of the increasing sexualization, including pornification, of our culture. This is one reason that, as I started to suggest in the Introduction, recent feminist media scholarship has attempted to grasp how it has come to be that for many contemporary women, sexual self-objectification is the new feminism.

One of the aims of this chapter is to tackle this question, to outline the story of how we've moved from a time—not so long ago—when women actively complained about the ways in which the mass media reduces them to sex objects to a time when many women believe that sexual self-objectification is a sign of female empowerment. How have we transitioned from feminism to a culture where "girl power" entails flashing your boobs to a drunken crowd of spring breakers just because they cheer loudly enough? More broadly speaking, I want to ask how we've arrived at today's confusing universe of gender and sexuality. In the second half of this chapter, we'll learn that twenty-first-century feminist media scholarship provides some answers through its analysis of neoliberalism, postfeminism, and the emergence of hyperfemininity. But first we need to make an excursion to psychoanalysis and psychoanalytic film theory.

Freud the feminist?

Over the years of teaching undergraduates, I've found that unless they're majoring in film studies or related theoretical fields, they know next to nothing about psychoanalysis. In addition, perhaps because the one thing that they *do* seem to know about it is that Sigmund Freud, the founder of psychoanalysis, accused women of suffering from penis envy, they tend to assume that it's an intrinsically misogynistic endeavor. Consequently, it can be difficult to explain to them why feminist film critics of the 1970s and 1980s became so fascinated by psychoanalysis and why many contemporary feminist critics continue to rely heavily on its insights. It may then be useful to start with the basics, including the fact that, whatever Freud's misconceptions about female sexuality—and there is no denying that, like most thinkers of his time, he had some drastic ones—he was well ahead of his nineteenth-century cultural milieu in acknowledging that, like men, women are sexual creatures.

The culture of Freud's time tended to view women as angelic beings with no sexual desire whatsoever. Freud, in contrast, found plenty of evidence of female sexuality in his clinical practice, which he developed largely on the basis of his experiences with hysterical female patients. The term "hysterical" today carries a derogatory tone, implying excessive (and unfounded) emotionality. Although this was sometimes part of Freud's definition as well, he used the term more broadly to designate an array of pathological symptoms, some of which were physical, such as the loss of sensation in a limb or the sudden inability to drink water.[2] Because the crux of Freud's interpretative practice was to trace the formation of such symptoms to sexual repression, he came to believe that the excessive curtailment of female sexuality that characterized his society was making women ill. In this manner, though Freud was certainly no feminist, he offered an important starting point for later feminist challenges to heteropatriarchal definitions of female sexuality.

Along related lines, Freud recognized that human sexuality is not a natural "given" but rather the result of a lengthy—and in many ways brutal—process of socialization. As opposed to evolutionary thinkers who emphasize the continuities between the sexual behavior of humans and other animals, Freud saw that sexuality is not an exception to the profoundly social tone of human life; he understood that the fact that humans live in a complex cultural world of norms, customs, economies, governments, universities, nightclubs, books, and so on, makes it difficult to draw direct comparisons between humans and other animals.

Even when it comes to basic bodily needs, such as eating or going to the bathroom, human actions are influenced by culture. When we're hungry, we often sit down at a table with dishes, glasses, forks, and knives to eat food that has been meticulously prepared; under normal circumstances, we refrain from spitting olive pits at each other. And when we need to use the bathroom at our boss's house, we discreetly close the door. What made Freud such a pioneering thinker is that he realized that our sexual behavior is guided by similar cultural dictates, which explains, for example, why most people don't want to have sex in broad daylight in the middle of a busy street. Most importantly for our purposes, Freud illustrated that human sexuality is entirely different from the reproductive instinct of other animals—that, among other things, it's driven by unconscious motivations that have little to do with the urge to bring children into the world.

Consider the following: not only is human sexual behavior deeply ritualistic, frequently (though not invariably) falling into socially determined configurations but also humans routinely reject sexual partners who are easily obtainable, reaching instead for ones who are uninterested or otherwise unavailable. In addition, humans tend to spend long stretches of time mourning lovers they've lost, and this can be the case even when they've been callously rejected by these lovers. This is a markedly ineffective way of going about the demands of reproduction, which is one reason that evolutionary comparisons between chimps and humans always seem to miss something fundamental. Freud, in contrast, was good at illustrating how the human infant's disorganized erotic drives over time become organized into a form of adult sexuality that is at once socially intelligible (makes at least some sense to other people) and rooted in highly irrational fixations of desire, fixations that often don't make sense even to the person who suffers from them.

The irrational fixations of desire have to do with its partially unconscious character. But what concerns us more immediately is that the development of normative (culturally condoned) adult sexuality entails the naturalization of heterosexuality and the normalization of complementary male and female roles, with the result that many people in our society come to think of gender-bifurcated heterosexuality as the only possible sexual arrangement.[3] Freud, who recognized that humans have the capacity for a variety of alternative sexual expressions, including homosexuality, took it upon himself to clarify how these alternative expressions are suppressed by a cultural machinery dedicated to the production of heterosexuality. This doesn't mean that Freud's comments on homosexuality were consistently unbiased. But his analysis of the social fashioning of gender-normative heterosexuality offered feminist theorists—and later, queer critics—some basic material to work with.

At the core of Freud's explanation of how the child's rudimentary eroticism is converted into socially acceptable adult sexuality stands the Oedipus complex. Freud proposed that, like Oedipus in Sophocles's *Oedipus Rex*, the (male) child initially loves his mother and wants to kill his father. But unlike Sophocles's Oedipus, who sleeps with his mother and murders his father, the child is prevented from carrying out his wishes by social norms that communicate that the fulfillment of these wishes would result in severe punishment: castration. The boy thus agrees to forgo his mother as a love object in exchange for keeping his penis. And he sublimates his murderous impulses toward his father into sentiments of identification and idealization, wanting, essentially, to grow up to be just like dad.

Freud's account may sound like science fiction—I find that most of my students at first find it preposterous—so it may help to know that, during Freud's time, it was common for parents to threaten little boys with castration when they misbehaved.[4] It may also help to think about the Oedipal story—with its interplay of love and hate—as a metaphor for the kinds of intense emotional attachments that children develop to their parents (or other caretakers) at an early age. Indeed, because children depend on their caretakers for their very survival, they don't have any choice but to develop such attachments, and this is the case even when their caretakers treat them badly. Love and hate are therefore built into the human psyche very early on, which is one reason that these sentiments tend to cause so much havoc throughout our lives; it can be difficult to break blueprints of loving and hating—of relating—that were internalized at such a tender age.

The blueprints of relating that children internalize are gendered. This is why Freud viewed the Oedipus complex as a tool of socialization that teaches little boys and girls to enact normative masculinity and femininity. Moreover, he was particularly intrigued by the female Oedipus complex,[5] which seemed to demand some counterintuitive psychic maneuvers, such as accepting the inferior position that, in Freud's heteropatriarchal society, automatically came with normative femininity. Because men in Freud's society enjoyed obvious privileges, it made sense for the little boy to want to become like his father. But Freud couldn't see any reward for adopting the culturally denigrated position of femininity. As a consequence, he kept banging his head against "the riddle of femininity," famously asking, "What does a woman want."[6]

Let us unpack the "feminine" dilemma a bit more. Freud saw that Western society codes the possessor of the penis (the man) as "having" something while coding the one who doesn't possess the penis (the woman) as "lacking" something. Instead of admitting that women have their own perfectly functioning sexual organs, the dominant cultural imagination envisions the absence of a penis as a gaping wound, as the kind of castration, deficiency, or deprivation that nothing can redeem. From this, there is merely a tiny leap to the idea that man—the one who "has" something—is an active subject whereas woman—the one who "lacks"—is a passive object: a nonsubject who requires completion by the subject, a.k.a. the man.

Penis envy, anyone?

Hell, yes! It would be bizarre to be a woman in such a cultural order and *not* envy the possessor of the penis. It's not that women necessarily want the penis itself—as to whether or not it's an attractive organ remains debatable—but who wouldn't want the social, political, and economic power associated with it? (In a moment, we'll discover that this power is in many ways illusory but this is a different story.) This is why Freud thought that it was reasonable for the little boy to emerge from the Oedipus complex willing to accept the role that society had reserved for him: not sleeping with his mother and not killing his father seemed like a small price to pay for eventually becoming like his (socially revered) father. But Freud was right in thinking that women's willingness to step into the position of the socially disparaged "other"—the one who is always already castrated—needed some explanation.

Freud, thus, couldn't understand why women didn't refuse the questionable title of the one who lacks. Overt oppression obviously played a significant role. But it couldn't entirely account for the prevalence of women's resignation to their inferior status. The explanation for this lack of rebellion lies in the very direction that Freud himself started to chart with his notion of the Oedipus complex: the process of socialization that produces normative masculinity and femininity. I'll return to this process below. Here it's enough to note that Freud wasn't able to push his analysis beyond the Oedipus complex, in part, because a more nuanced understanding of the cultural (re)production of gender demanded theoretical tools that he didn't yet have access to, such as twentieth-century insights regarding the socially constructed nature of subjectivity.

This is why it was left to later thinkers, including contemporary feminist and queer theorists, to complete the picture of how our society persuades women to consent to, and even take pleasure in, their position as a nonsubject (an object). But Freud already had a fairly solid grasp on what Simone de Beauvoir, in *The Second Sex* (1949), famously summed up as follows: "One is not born, but rather becomes, woman."[7] He already understood that femininity is something that women painstakingly learn through a rigorous process of socialization. In part because Freud, like all thinkers, was to some extent hemmed in by the social norms of his culture, his commentary on femininity at times veered toward social platitudes. Yet, he also tried harder than most thinkers of his time—or even of our own—to avoid the pitfalls of stereotypical thinking, which is why, though he was not a feminist, many feminists have a soft spot for him.

Jacques Lacan: Lack, desire, fantasy

The French psychoanalyst Jacques Lacan was no more a feminist than Freud, but it was his inspired interpretation of Freudian theory, starting in the 1950s, and reaching the Anglo-American academy by the early 1970s, that convinced many feminist critics to take Freud seriously. Lacan combined Freudian psychoanalysis with structuralist linguistics and anthropology—particularly the work of Ferdinand de Saussure and Claude Lévi-Strauss—to devise an account of subject formation, of how we become who we are, that became one of the most influential components of late-twentieth-century theory.

For Lacan, "castration" in the sense of feeling wounded, deficient, or deprived of something is a general condition of human subjectivity. Although he agreed with Freud that in our society it's woman in particular who is asked to perform the role of the one who "lacks" something essential (the penis), he asserted that in reality lack—feeling castrated, feeling like a part of us has been sliced of and lost—is the price we all, men as much as women, pay for becoming subjects capable of participating in collective social life, in what he called "the symbolic order." More specifically, Lacan hypothesized that there is something about the process of learning to speak—which is how children enter the symbolic order—that instills a sense of deprivation and inadequacy at the core of subjectivity. If the infant who doesn't yet speak also doesn't yet recognize itself as separate from the world (say, from its mother), the child who begins to speak quickly learns to make distinctions, including the distinction between itself and the rest of the world. This in turn leads to the child's realization that far from being the center of the universe, he's merely a tiny cog in its immense machinery, a machinery over which he, furthermore, has virtually no control. This is a humbling recognition, generating a feeling of dispossession that nothing can redeem.

In this way, Lacan universalized castration, suggesting that the mutilation that the little boy fears in the Freudian Oedipal scenario is something that all of us, metaphorically speaking, experience. Moreover, by the time we're cognitively able to worry about it, it has already happened. We may not be physically mutilated (castrated), but we experience ourselves as psychically mutilated (lacking) in ways that we can't fully name. We may spend much of our lives fleeing from our lack—finding various ways to distract ourselves from our deficiency—but there are moments in most human lives when it leaps to the forefront of our consciousness, particularly during times of suffering. This is yet another way that humans (presumably) differ from other animals: as Western philosophy has repeatedly illustrated, humans spend a great deal of energy worrying about all the ways in which they don't feel whole.

Lacan aligns the lack at the heart of human life with the birth of desire. Simply put, our sense of lack gives rise to attempts to fill it, which is what desire ultimately consists of. We reach into the world in quest of various objects, ambitions, and occupations that we hope will enable us to regain the wholeness we imagine having lost. However, Lacan specifies that our impression of having been deprived of something unfathomably precious is a fantasy, that we haven't actually lost anything but have merely invented—after the fact—an image of past plenitude that we assume we once possessed and that we're desperate to recover. This in turn means that there is no surefire way to quench our desire: because we haven't in reality lost anything, there is no object, ambition, or occupation that can definitively cure our longing.

That said, we can usually find satisfactions that offer us partial compensation, that cause our lack—even if just temporarily—to recede to the background. As you might guess, movies are an effective means of distracting ourselves (more on this momentarily). Falling in love is another common distraction. It gives us the impression that our lack has finally been filled, our wound healed, and our castration annulled. In due time, even this fantasy often collapses. But as a provisional coping strategy, falling in love can be quite effective.

It's worth emphasizing that our society's insistence on complementary gender roles aids in the fabrication of the fantasy of redemption through romance. Traditionally, it was thought that women, by remaining in the private domain, soothed away the anxieties that accrued to men in the public domain; woman was to be the caretaker, the redeemer of men who, without her humanizing touch, might become overly callous and selfish. In other words, even though our society's most fundamental conviction about men and women is that women (as embodiments of lack) need men to complete them (to fill their lack, both literally and figuratively), it also—conveniently, one might add—imagines that women possess qualities (say, empathy and emotional intelligence) that help ease men's burden of competing in the public sphere.

In this manner, our heteropatriarchal culture devises a mythology of gender complementarity in which men and women are capable of saving each other: women are rescued by men's ambition, activities, and protection whereas men are rescued by women's tender sensibilities. Today, too many women participate in the work force to make their role as guardians of the hearth tenable. Yet even this hasn't eradicated the notion that it's women's task to salvage men emotionally, as is obvious from countless movie plots—including that of *Pretty Woman*—that portray an emotionally closed man who is gradually brought to life by a woman.

Even though Lacan's account of lack offers one explanation for why this mythology of gender complementarity remains so intractable in our society, he himself ridiculed it, viewing it as one of the ways in which our culture tries to fool us into thinking that there is a remedy for our ontological (and existential) malaise. This is one reason feminists have gravitated toward his theory. In addition, feminists have profited from his illustration of how culture—through language and other signifying systems—creates gendered meaning out of anatomical difference. For instance, in the course of one of his lectures, he drew two identical doors, which he then labeled "gentlemen" and "ladies." His point was that it's not the doors that generate a gender binary—for they are identical—but rather the words (signifiers) placed on those doors.[8] Likewise, penis, vagina, and other anatomical characteristics don't in themselves mean anything in particular; rather, it's the social assumptions imposed on these characteristics that produce (heteropatriarchal) meaning.

Like Freud, Lacan recognized that our society elevates the penis to a special status, granting its possessor privileges that it denies those who lack it. But Lacan went further than Freud in theorizing the entirely illusory status of these privileges: the fact that no one—not even the guy with the biggest dick—can possibly live up to the ideal of phallic power that underpins heteropatriarchy as a system of male dominance. On some level, we know this, which is why we make fun of the enormous belt buckles, cowboy hats, and red convertibles that some men resort to in order to reassure themselves of their manly (phallic) status. Lacan succinctly named the desperation beneath this charade when he argued that the phallus as a signifier of social power has no referent in the real world, that the penis doesn't equal the phallus, no matter how much some men would like this to be the case.[9]

That said, because men possess the penis, and because our society tends to automatically conflate the penis with phallic power, men arguably find it easier than women do to delude themselves into thinking that they're not lacking. Masculine peacocking is one way to attain this goal, to deny the lack—the foundational castration—that characterizes every human life. By this I don't mean to imply that the social oppression of women isn't real, that it doesn't have any concrete consequences—for obviously it does—but merely that, in Lacanian terms, masculine displays of authority amount to a futile attempt to erase the fact that, at the end of the day, men are just as fragmented, just as torn up, as women are.

The power of cinematic suture

Before outlining some of the ways that feminist film theory has appropriated Freudian and Lacanian insights about the constitution of masculinity and femininity, I want to note that Lacan's theorization of lack provides a compelling way to understand cinematic suture: the phenomenon of spectators being drawn into the filmic narrative so seamlessly that they forget that they're watching an illusory world. In *The Subject of Semiotics* (1983), Kaja Silverman proposes that screen images have this power over us because they promise to heal—precisely, to suture—the gaping hole within our being. Like an adored object of love, screen images give us something concrete to hold onto so that we can temporarily forget about the deficiencies of life (and of our own being). In part this is because our ability to identify with the idealized characters on the screen offers us narcissistic gratification. But in part it's because there is something about the unfolding of the narrative itself—its movement toward resolution—that satisfies our need for closure, that speaks to the fantasy of regained wholeness that Lacan diagnosed as one of the key elements of the human condition.

The resolution of conflicts is one of the trademarks of mainstream movies. What's more, insofar as such movies offer us conventional plot lines, they give us the satisfaction of knowing from the get-go how things are going to turn out; we may not be able to foresee every plot twist but we have a ballpark understanding of where the characters will end up. For example, when watching a romantic comedy such as *Pretty Woman*, we know not only that the heroine won't die but also that, whatever the trials she undergoes during the narrative, she'll eventually triumph. We also know that the hero of the story isn't going to rape or beat up the heroine, that—whatever his flaws—he'll eventually turn out to be a decent chap. And we know that no matter how much the hero and the heroine bicker, the movie will end with a reconciliation and the promise of romantic fulfillment.

There are mainstream movies—and particularly recent television shows—that break some of our basic expectations, so that, for instance, the television series *24* (2006–14) shocked audiences by routinely killing off its main characters (except, of course, its hero Jack Bauer, who had the ability to overcome even his own death). At the start of the series, this practice was lauded as an innovation, and it has since been adopted by other popular series, such as *The Good Wife* (2009–), *Downton Abbey* (2010–), *Homeland* (2011–), and even the teen hit *The Vampire Diaries* (2009–). Contemporary television knows how to raise the stakes by derailing the spectator's expectations. However, many movie genres seem untouchable in this regard because it would be inconceivable, say, to end a romantic comedy with the heroine's death. There are of course movies aimed at female audiences that subvert conventions, that in one way or another deny the happy ending audiences anticipate. But these are not "pure" romantic comedies. Spectators know that when they watch a romcom directed by Garry Marshall, Nancy Meyers, or Nora Ephron, they'll get their happy ending.

Silverman maintains that "we want suture so badly that we'll take it at any price."[10] This means, among other things, that we're willing to tolerate delays in narrative closure. Such delays in fact only whet our appetite for suture, so that we put up with unanticipated plot twists in the hope that in the end things will be resolved to our satisfaction. This is why we keep watching a show like *The Good Wife* even after it has killed off its leading man, thereby extinguishing the possibility that the female protagonist will end up with him. In a way, the excruciating disruption of suture creates an even greater need for it; the temporary scrambling of codes—the temporary manufacture of turmoil, disarray, and confusion—makes the final restoration of order all the more gratifying.

Early feminist analyses of suture—including that of Silverman—tended to focus on its problematic side, namely that the reason it's so effective in drawing us into various fantasy worlds is that it relies on easily recognizable archetypes, including gender stereotypes. In other words, suture presupposes our willingness to accept conventional depictions of gender. What's more, such conventional depictions reassure us that our society's interpretation of the world is correct, thereby reinforcing the lived realities of gender. As Silverman asserts, through suture "the subject emerges within discourse, and (at least ideally) takes up a position congruent with the existing cultural order."[11] That is, when watching a mainstream movie, we're inserted into a familiar—and therefore instantly comforting—nexus of (gendered) meaning. When we identify with the (gendered) role that this nexus of meaning offers us, we discover our "rightful" place within our society: we "emerge" as a subject in ways that are immediately readable by others.

Silverman posits that not only does suture help us "emerge" as a subject by giving us a clear model for who we're supposed to be but it also helps sustain—repeatedly "reactivate"—our subjectivity over time.[12] Teresa de Lauretis expresses the same idea more concretely in her 1984 *Alice Doesn't*: "If women spectators are to buy their tickets and their popcorn, the work of cinema ... may be said to require women's consent; and we may well suspect that narrative cinema in particular must be aimed, like desire, toward seducing women into femininity."[13] De Lauretis, in short, believes that women must be cunningly seduced into femininity—constantly "reactivated" as feminine subjects in Silverman's sense—if the heteropatriarchal social order is to survive. Suture, particularly the display of glamorous images of femininity on screen, is the cinematic mechanism that accomplishes this reactivation, that ensures that, as de Lauretis puts it, women are "made again and again" as women.[14]

The accounts of Silverman and de Lauretis provide one explanation for the riddle of femininity that frustrated Freud. They imply—as Freud already did—that the parameters of normative femininity are so objectionable that women must be given compelling reasons for their complicity with the system; they must, precisely, be seduced into femininity. Suture in turn serves as one of the instruments of this seduction, as a way of convincing women that being a nonsubject—a passive object of desire—is pleasurable. As we'll see momentarily, later theories of spectatorship insist on a greater degree of distance between spectators and movie narratives, claiming that spectators aren't mere passive dupes of dominant cultural codes but rather active participants in the creation (and revision) of these codes. Still, the analysis of suture undertaken by psychoanalytic feminist film theorists of the 1980s went some way in explaining the reproduction of normative femininity in our culture.

"Femininity" as a heteropatriarchal invention

Feminist film theorists thus employed Freudian-Lacanian psychoanalysis to illustrate the power of movies to suture us into their narratives, including ones that communicate questionable messages about gender. But perhaps even more importantly, they attempted to shed light on the ways in which movies generate gendered messages in the first place;

they sought to tease out the full implications of the idea that masculinity and femininity are not biological givens—innate characteristics of men and women—but rather products of a society organized around phallic power. If Freud focused on the Oedipus complex as a tool of gender socialization, feminist critics were, more generally, interested in how dominant codes of gender and sexuality become internalized to such a degree that they're experienced as entirely taken-for-granted components of our subjectivity.

Gender socialization often starts before birth in the sense that many parents decorate nurseries and purchase toys based on the gender of the child they're expecting, so that when the child arrives, he or she immediately encounters either a blue world of model trains, race cars, and Lego sets or a pink world of Barbie dolls, stuffed animals, and miniature tea sets. The little child doesn't have much of a chance against these worlds. Some children of course rebel. And not all parents want to participate in this convention. But, overall, gender conditioning is virtually impossible to escape: if it doesn't start at home, then kindergarten, elementary school, and the rest of society will in time accomplish it. Importantly, children realize early on that deviations from normative gender scripts will be punished: they don't need to be threatened with castration to understand that nonconformity will result in social ostracization and ridicule.

These days, more and more people are able to resist our culture's dominant gender codes. But their resistance doesn't usually materialize until they're teenagers (and sometimes even middle-aged adults, as was the case with Bruce Jenner, now Caitlyn Jenner). Most of us undergo gender socialization largely unconsciously. This means that when normative gender codes are internalized, they become so deeply embedded in our inner lives—and even in our bodily way of inhabiting the world (walking, sitting, eating, smiling, and so on)—that we come to think of them as who we, quite simply, "are"; we completely lose track of the fact that what is now inside was once outside of us, assuming that the characteristics that now feel so "right" to us arise from the depths of our being.

A common misconception about the nature versus nurture debate is that the results of nurture are easier to change than the results of nature. This isn't necessarily the case. Socially generated forms of behavior—including gendered behavior—are so thoroughly incorporated into our self-understanding that altering them would be akin to becoming a wholly different person. This is why we often adhere to them even when they oppress us. It's one reason women don't always rebel against the constraints of normative femininity even when these constraints exasperate them.

Let me restate the obvious: historically—and to some degree even today—gender socialization has served the needs of a heteropatriarchal society that has a stake in preserving both the primacy of heterosexuality and gender inequality. By this I don't mean that men as a group are deliberately plotting to keep women down—though there are some men who might go this far—but rather that on the structural level, our society is male-centered (phallocentric), and that the momentum of this society unfolds in semiautomatic ways, without anyone holding the reins, to reproduce the models of masculinity and femininity that support its overall logic. This is why Ann Kaplan notes in *Feminism and Film* (2000) that, outside of heteropatriarchal constructs, "it is impossible to know what the feminine might be."[15]

This is a key observation: femininity is a heteropatriarchal *invention*. On the one hand, patriarchy also constructs (and constrains) men: it forces both men and women into suffocating gender-specific boxes. On the other, because of the historical power differential between men and women, femininity has over the centuries been molded in ways that are designed to meet male needs more than vice versa. This explains why women have been hypersexualized at the same time as their sexuality has been severely restrained.

The paradox here is only apparent, for heteropatriarchy benefits not only from overt displays of female sexuality but also from the (simultaneous) disciplining of this sexuality. In addition, women have traditionally been asked to undertake the tedious task of reinforcing masculine fantasies of autonomy: by stepping into their culturally designated position as the one who "lacks," women have bolstered men's confidence in their "wholeness," in their intactness as human beings as well as in their ability to accomplish things; women, in short, have offered men narcissistic satisfaction. As Virginia Woolf wryly observes, women have over the centuries been asked to reflect back to man an image of himself twice his size.[16]

Post feminism, things have improved so that we now live in a much more egalitarian culture. Most Western women do not see themselves as subordinate to men, and perhaps they have, for the most part, genuinely been freed from the task of playing a supporting role in men's narcissistic pursuits. Yet traces of the old order persist, and perhaps nowhere as strongly as in our society's visual iconography, which still clearly portrays femininity as a heteropatriarchal invention. The restrictions on female sexuality may have loosened but the practice of female sexual objectification has arguably only intensified.

We're all familiar with the image of the perfect woman: the woman staring at us from billboards and magazine covers, the one with pouty, silicon-enhanced lips; perky, silicon-enhanced breasts; and a rounded, silicon-enhanced butt. We know that this image has been airbrushed. And we know that it's the full-time job of the woman in this image to look amazing. But we still can't keep the image from insinuating itself into our psychic lives.

This woman is a fantasy object that has little to do with actual women. She's the modern version of the mythological Woman, the Icon of Femininity, that has always existed in one form or other. Like the phallus, this Woman has no real-life referent: she's the feminine equivalent of the masculine fantasy of perfection (or power) that the phallus symbolizes but that no one can actually embody.[17] Hollywood makes up for this impossibility by breathing life into these fantasy creatures so that, for the duration of the movie, we get to pretend that our culture's ideals of masculinity and femininity are tangible (walking, talking) entities.

These days, movies sometimes engage in gender blending so that Angelina Jolie, for instance, routinely gets to assassinate a battalion of villains while simultaneously looking like she has stepped out of the pages of *Vogue*. But, generally speaking, one of the most prominent features of Hollywood has always been its capacity to map our culture's ideals of masculinity and femininity onto (gendered) bodies that appear to incarnate these ideals in relatively pure form. This is why psychoanalytic feminist film critics have taken a special interest in the relationship between Hollywood film and the so-called "patriarchal unconscious": the collective unconscious belief systems that govern male-dominated society. Kaplan, for example, asserts that "film narratives, like dreams, symbolize a latent, repressed content, only now the 'content' refers not to an individual unconscious but to that of patriarchy in general. If psychoanalysis is a tool that will unlock the meaning of dreams, it should also unlock that of films."[18]

Kaplan thus believes that the techniques of interpretation, such as dream analysis, that Freud developed to explore the individual unconscious can also be used to expose the logic of movies as an expression of our society's collective (patriarchal) unconscious. Along closely related lines, Laura Mulvey declares with a degree of feminist belligerence: "Psychoanalytic theory is ... appropriated here as a political weapon, demonstrating the way the unconscious of patriarchal society has structured film form."[19] Both critics are convinced that psychoanalysis can teach us something about the basic functioning of heteropatriarchy. More specifically, both are interested in understanding how cinematographic conventions and techniques are used to produce the seductive image of the perfect Woman as well as to display this image for the male gaze.

The male gaze

I noted at the beginning of this chapter that women in our society have been taught to think of themselves as enticing objects for male desire. Within the visual world of the movies, as (frequently) in the real world, this means that men look at women whereas women display themselves for the male gaze.[20] As Mulvey remarks in the context of classic Hollywood cinema:

> In a world ordered by sexual imbalance, pleasure in looking has been split between active/male and passive/female. The determining male gaze projects its fantasy onto the female figure, which is stylized accordingly. In their traditional exhibitionist role women are simultaneously looked at and displayed, with their appearance coded for strong visual and erotic impact so that they can be said to connote *to-be-looked-at-ness*.[21]

In a moment, I'll outline some of the ways in which Mulvey's rendering of the play of desire has been challenged by later critics. But this statement from her 1975 essay, "Visual Pleasure and Narrative Cinema," is one of the most legendary pronouncements of feminist film theory, conveying the point about the organization of desire under heteropatriarchy that I've flagged as an ongoing concern for contemporary feminist media scholarship. This point is worth reiterating: insofar as men are active subjects of desire whereas women are merely its passive objects, the only form of desire available to women is the desire to be desired: the desire to become the perfect object of desire for the male gaze. In other words, women's desire is indirect, so that the closest they come to feeling desire is desiring men's desire; essentially, they want to be wanted. In this manner, women's eroticism is constructed around their own objectification. As Kaplan starkly claims, women's "positioning as 'to-be-looked-at,' as object of the gaze, has . . . come to be sexually pleasurable."[22]

In teaching feminist film theory, I've found this to be a sobering insight for many young women, for they instantly recognize the continued relevance of Mulvey's articulation of women's desire to be desired. To be sure, things have changed since 1975: today's billboards, magazines, television shows, and Hollywood movies are filled with men who are displayed—frequently half-naked—for the straight female gaze; it's now okay for women to look at men, objectify them, desire them, and so on. Indeed, acknowledging active female desire has become one of the most successful advertising tricks of the twenty-first century, second only to the trope of "female empowerment" that is used to sell us everything from clothes, makeup, and perfume to cars and condos.

At the same time, women are still in many ways expected to signal their desirability rather than to approach the object of their desire directly; they're expected to send (usually discreet) intimations of availability in the hope that the man they're interested in will act on these signals and approach them. As a result, as much as we might want to think that the days of relegating women to objects of the male gaze are over, the imprint of this dynamic persists: a woman is asked to (more or less) passively wait for a man to decide if she's desirable enough to be pursued.

Street harassment is one of the most obvious ways in which our society signals to women that, when it comes to the male gaze, they don't have any choice but to submit to it: any man, at any time, appears to possess the right to publicly assess a woman's desirability and to even comment on it out loud. There is no doubt that women can play into the male gaze, that women sometimes feel empowered when they know that they're galvanizing this gaze, as may, for example, be the case when they walk into a party knowing that they look fantastic. But the flip side of such moments of empowerment are the moments on the street when some random guy feels that it's his God-given right to appraise your physique.

What gives him this right? Centuries of heteropatriarchal tradition that have taught men that this right is theirs by virtue of being men (in this sense Freud was entirely justified in implying that the penis means quite a bit in our culture, that it might be the epicenter of symbolic power around which everything else is forced to pivot). These days, many men deliberately reject this dynamic, wanting nothing to do with the legacies of heteropatriarchy. Conversely, some women eagerly participate in the system not only by inviting the male gaze but also by turning their own critical gaze toward other women, explicitly evaluating the desirability of these women according to criteria set by heteropatriarchy. Consequently, the next time you catch yourself judging a woman in some café—is that outfit flattering? do her shoes match her jacket? is she thin enough? look at those boobs! is she more attractive than me?—you might want to ask yourself whose eyes you are looking through.

This was one of the first questions that psychoanalytic feminist film critics—most notably Mulvey—asked about the female spectator of classic Hollywood cinema. Mulvey proposed that within the parameters of this cinema, the male gaze is activated through three "looks": (1) the look of the camera (which positions women on screen to-be-looked-at); (2) the look of the men within the movie's narrative (how men on screen look at women on screen); and (3) the look of the audience, which tends to automatically align itself with the male protagonist—the agent of action on the screen—so that spectators, regardless of gender, identify with the protagonist's point of view, seeing things, including the women he assesses, as he sees them.

For instance, in Hitchcock's *Vertigo* (1958)—which Mulvey uses to illustrate her argument—male and female viewers alike are induced to identify with the perspective of the male protagonist, private investigator Scottie Ferguson (Jimmy Stewart), who is hired to solve the mystery of a beautiful woman called Madeleine (Kim Novak). This plot line gives Scottie ample opportunity to watch Madeleine—with whom he becomes increasingly obsessed—from a distance, with the consequence that she's explicitly positioned as a passive object of his inquisitive gaze. Moreover, the film uses various techniques to establish the dominance of Scottie's point of view, such as a lengthy shot-reverse shot sequence during which Scottie secretly trails Madeleine through the streets of San Francisco: we get a close-up of Scottie's face behind the wheel of his car; next we get a long-shot of Madeleine's car; then we get another close-up of Scottie; another long-shot of Madeleine, and so on, until there is no way to avoid the sensation of observing Madeleine through Scottie's eyes. Essentially, we're forced into the position of a voyeur in relation to the female object of desire.

Mulvey's general point is that classic Hollywood cinema tends to be so seamlessly organized around the male gaze that female spectators are left with two equally unpalatable choices: either they need to adopt the male gaze, looking at women on the screen from the male perspective; or they can identify with the women on the screen, thereby accepting their status as passive objects of the gaze. The first choice is aligned with sadism—understood in this context as the drive to subjugate the object of one's desire to a scrutinizing, even aggressive gaze—whereas the second, unfortunately for female spectators, is aligned with masochism: submission to the controlling gaze of the other.

Mulvey believes that to the extent that male protagonists in Hollywood cinema control both the action and the women within the narrative, male viewers get to indulge in a relatively straightforward identification: they get to identify with an idealized version of themselves. Female viewers, in contrast, can either identify with the men on the screen (thereby giving up their identity as women) or with the women on the screen, particularly with these women's capacity to fascinate men. Whenever they opt for the latter identification, they learn to take pleasure in their own objectification; they learn to take pleasure in the idea that, like their female alter egos on the screen, they might one day be able to arouse men's desire by incarnating the mythological Woman of heteropatriarchal fantasy.

Mulvey's analysis thus suggests that Hollywood cinema—like much of the rest of our culture—teaches straight women to covet the opportunity to become objects of the male gaze because this is the only way that they can attain any degree of agency: the limited control they wield over men through their sexuality. Though it may well be that objectification is inherent to eroticism, that every object of desire is intrinsically to some degree objectified, the patriarchal unconscious creates a gendered division of labor where straight women's pleasure arises from their *own* objectification rather than from the objectification of men.

The male gaze revisited

One can see why Mulvey's theory of the male gaze constitutes one of the most enduring innovations of feminist film theory. Yet, as many later critics have pointed out, it's also somewhat reductive. A closer look at *Vertigo* will demonstrate why, for the movie is too intelligent to play out the gendered game of heteropatriarchy as straightforwardly as Mulvey's account implies. *Vertigo* also deserves a closer look because it will serve as a comparison point to *Pretty Woman* in the next chapter.

At first glance, *Vertigo* certainly confirms the heteropatriarchal nightmare that Mulvey analyzes, namely that women can only elicit male desire by impersonating the mythological Woman with the capital W. Hitchcock achieves this effect by presenting Scottie with two versions of the same woman. Recall Scottie's obsession with the elusive Madeleine whose mystery he has been hired to solve? Well, midway through the movie, Scottie ends up in a mental hospital after he witnesses what he thinks is Madeleine's death. What the audience learns well before Scottie does is that this death was faked by a woman called Judy who had been hired to impersonate Madeleine by the latter's husband (in order to hide the fact that he had killed the "real" Madeleine). In other words, the audience recognizes that the woman Scottie has fallen head over heels for was never Madeleine to begin with but rather Judy. Madeleine's "death" was merely Judy's last "act" as Madeleine.

After Scottie is released from the mental hospital, he runs into Judy on the street. Not realizing that he's interacting with the same women who earlier mesmerized him as Madeleine, but intrigued by the faint resemblance between the two women, Scottie starts to tentatively date Judy. But sadly, Judy, whose own "look" is much less refined than the look she donned while pretending to be the elegant Madeleine, simply just doesn't do it for him. Judy—who is by now in love with Scottie—finds that she's unable to ignite Scottie's desire without the clothes, hair style, and makeup that allowed her to captivate Scottie's interest when she played the stylish Madeleine. What Scottie wants is the fantasy object that Madeleine represented for him.

As opposed to Madeleine, whose personality remained obscure, Judy is too down-to-earth, too "real," to satisfy Scottie's fantasy. In this manner, Hitchcock demonstrates that the fantasy of feminine perfection that heteropatriarchy produces can only be sustained at a distance: when the woman become too proximate, too familiar, she ceases to charm. Scottie's perfect Woman, like the perfect Woman of so many male protagonists of Hollywood movies, is not merely beautiful but also inscrutable and inaccessible.

Scottie is so fixated on his fantasy that he embarks on a mission of turning Judy into Madeleine. Judy initially protests this attempt to stifle her character. But after she recognizes her impotence in comparison to the fantasy of polished femininity that Scottie is after, she reluctantly consents to reviving her role as Madeleine. What follows is one of the most chilling makeover sequences in movie history, as we watch Judy undergo a thorough transformation—consisting of a new wardrobe, hair color, and style of makeup—in order to once again embody Scottie's ideal.

Particularly poignant is a shopping scene that foreshadows *Pretty Woman* in important ways: Scottie accompanies Judy to an expensive department store where he handpicks her outfits for her over her loud protestations. These outfits are identical to the ones that Judy wore when she impersonated Madeleine, so she's fully aware of the fact that Scottie is trying to recreate his fantasy. Hitchcock's message about the power dynamics of heteropatriarchy couldn't be clearer: when Judy tries to resist the transformation, Scottie responds with an exasperated "It can't make that much of a difference to you."

This is why it's impossible to reduce *Vertigo* to Mulvey's reading. Hitchcock's characterization of Scottie's fixation on his fantasy woman is so deliberate that it's possible to argue that instead of teaching women to take pleasure in their own objectification—as Mulvey would have it—*Vertigo* offers an incisive commentary on the violence of heteropatriarchy. The shopping scene brilliantly discloses the degree to which masculine fantasy bypasses female subjectivity—any identity that a woman might have outside of this fantasy—by having Scottie insist, to the point of brutality, on the iconography of femininity that corresponds to the outlines of his fantasy. This scene illustrates that Scottie's fantasy is so important to him that when the world fails to deliver it, he sets out to manufacture it.

In her 1989 reassessment of Mulvey's interpretation of *Vertigo*, Karen Hollinger asserts that in detaching the male gaze from its narrative context—such as the uncomfortable shopping scene I've just described—Mulvey overlooks the possibility that, far from reaffirming heteropatriarchy, *Vertigo* exposes "the incompatibility of male desire and female individuality, independence, and emancipation."[23] By allowing spectators to witness Judy's torment as she struggles to suppress her personality in order to fulfill the specifications of Scottie's fantasy, and by rendering Scottie's gaze increasingly perverse, increasingly disturbing, the film destabilizes the spectator's ability to identify with him, so that by the end, the spectator may be as critical of the coerciveness of the male gaze as Mulvey herself is.

De Lauretis in turn strives to complexify Mulvey's argument by focusing on the ambivalences of female spectatorship. Despite the observations that de Lauretis makes about women being seduced into femininity that I outlined earlier, she concludes that female spectators of Hollywood films frequently form identifications across gender lines, aligning themselves with both the active male protagonist and his female object of desire. In other words, the idea that men invariably identify with the active gaze and women with the passive object of this gaze doesn't accurately capture the complex interplay of identifications that many spectators experience. Simply put, there is no direct correspondence between the gender of the viewer and the gender of the character who elicits identification, as is obvious to any female spectator who is used to identifying with the male protagonist of action movies.

The fact that it's hard to undo gender socialization doesn't mean that we're wholly locked into our predetermined location. Indeed, that we're not is one of the main principles of third-wave feminism—which I'll discuss below. For now, let me merely note that de Lauretis proposes that to the degree that masculinity and femininity are social "positions" that men and women occupy in relation to desire, they can never be "fully attained or fully relinquished."[24] That is, if none of us can ever entirely escape our culture's gender ideals, neither do we ever entirely coincide with them, with the result that we may possess the capacity to circle in and out of these ideals relatively fluidly; insofar as we understand that masculinity and femininity are ideals that don't correspond to male and female essences, that aren't intrinsically tied to bodies, we may—at least in the context of Hollywood fantasies—be able to exchange places, to slip into a slot that isn't "meant" for us but that we happen to like anyway.

bell hooks adds a black feminist perspective to the conversation by demonstrating that the assumption that female spectators will automatically submit to the male gaze presupposes a white audience. hooks posits that while white women may worry about being objectified by the male gaze, black women confront a world where this gaze frequently glides over them without making any note of them; in a nutshell, black women "don't count" according to dominant standards of attractiveness. This is not to say that black women are never objectified. Rather, hooks's point is that because our society is not just heteropatriarchal but also racist, black women can be rendered invisible by being excluded from mainstream ideals of femininity.

hooks proposes that this predicament can give rise to a politicized manner of engaging with filmic images where enjoyment doesn't arise from complacent suture but rather from a contestation of—and critical commentary on—such images. hooks calls this critical attitude "the oppositional gaze": a defiant gaze that counters the male gaze by actively challenging normative definitions of femininity.[25] As hooks sums up the matter, "Identifying with neither the phallocentric gaze nor the construction of white womanhood as lack, critical black female spectators construct a theory of looking relations where cinematic visual delight is the pleasure of interrogation."[26]

Such critiques of Mulvey's argument challenge the idea that spectators form easily classifiable identifications with cinematic images. Moreover, as Joan Copjec proposes in *Read My Desire* (1994), the notion of "identification" may not accurately reflect the dynamic between spectator and image in the first place.[27] In Copjec's view, cinematic images don't merely—or even primarily—facilitate our identification with gratifying alter egos but rather invite the investment of our desire. Desire, in turn, doesn't always manage to master its object in the way that the male gaze (in Mulvey's reading) does. Rather, desire often leads to a loss of mastery, even anxiety, so that the pleasure we take in movies cannot be understood simply as a function of our ability to use the movie screen as a mirror that grants us narcissistic satisfaction.

When the object looks back

Copjec's assertion that desire can decenter and even traumatize the subject, including the viewing subject, is connected to a more strictly Lacanian theory of the gaze than the one Mulvey presents. This theory has been developed by Lacanians such as Copjec herself, Todd McGowan, and Slavoj Žižek, who have been critical of the relatively simplistic ways in which Lacanian thought was appropriated by film theorists associated with the

British journal *Screen*, the journal that published Mulvey's 1975 essay.[28] If Mulvey—and other feminist film theorists who followed her lead—equates the gaze fairly straightforwardly with the (male) subject's act of looking, the later critics I've just named correctly point out that Lacan in fact associates the gaze with a disconcerting hole, or absence, within the subject's field of vision. This hole in turn is what generates the desire that, as McGowan puts it, "draws spectators into the cinema in the first place."[29]

McGowan explains that an all-seeing subject would have no desire to look. Rather, we desire to see because we can't see everything, because our field of vision is distorted by blank spots. The movie screen is one such blank spot. As McGowan remarks, "The screen that provides us something to look at simultaneously screens off a portion of what we can see"; instead of reflecting back to us an idealized image of ourselves that feeds our narcissistic sense of wholeness—as I, following Silverman, argued above—the screen in McGowan's account "carves out a hole in the field of vision," revealing to us that we aren't whole after all, that we aren't all seeing, "that there is no such thing as a God's eye view on reality."[30]

The movie screen both allows us to see and limits our field of vision, thereby inciting our desire to see more than we can. Moreover, the screen arguably looks at us as much as we look at it. In this sense, it's one version of what Lacan calls the gaze. But this is a gaze that—precisely insofar as it "carves out a hole" in our field of vision—disturbs and disrupts our vision even as it invites our attention. As McGowan clarifies, "The gaze is a distortion within the visual field, a point at which the seeming omnipotence of vision breaks down"; the gaze "appears in the guise of a blot that renders a portion of the visual field unintelligible."[31] In this sense, the Lacanian gaze is the very opposite of the mastering (male) gaze that Mulvey analyzes: the Lacanian gaze destroys mastery, bringing with it the impotence of unintelligibility.

Here it helps to consider an example that McGowan reproduces from one of Lacan's seminars.[32] Lacan tells a personal anecdote of how, when he was a young man looking for adventure, he left the safety of his cultured milieu to work with a group of fishermen in a French coastal town. Lacan remained a stranger in this working-class setting. When out at sea one day, a fisherman nicknamed Petit-Jean pointed to a sardine can gleaming in the ocean and told Lacan that even though Lacan could see the can, the can couldn't see Lacan. In so doing, Petit-Jean meant to indicate to Lacan that, like the sardine can that didn't belong in the ocean, Lacan didn't belong in the fishing village (perhaps Petit-Jean even meant to suggest that in relation to the village Lacan was as blind as a sardine can). But Lacan himself arrived at a different—albeit related—interpretation of the can, stating, "If what Petit-Jean said to me, namely, that the can did not see me, had any meaning, it was because in a sense, it was looking at me all the same."[33] McGowan glosses this as follows: "The sardine can looks at Lacan insofar as it distorts the ocean's surface in the same way that Lacan's own perspective and desire distorts life in the fishing village."[34]

The sardine can is a vaguely unsettling object that looks back, a blank spot in the ocean's surface that distorts this surface in the same way that Lacan distorts the surface of life in the fishing village; it's an uncanny entity that signifies that something is slightly off. Stated differently, the sardine can functions as the site of a disconcerting gaze in the same way that Lacan himself functions as the site of a (defective) gaze in relation to the fishing village: the decentering and traumatizing gaze of an outsider who disturbs the normal flow of daily existence.

The example of the sardine can implies that the gaze in the Lacanian sense emanates from an object that seems to look back at us even though we can't actually *see* its gaze. Žižek explains this dynamic as follows:

> Crucial for the Lacanian notion of Gaze is that it involves the reversal of the relationship between subject and object: as Lacan puts it in his *Seminar XI*, there is an antinomy

between the eye and the Gaze, i.e. the Gaze is on the side
of the object, it stands for the blind spot in the field of
the visible from which the picture itself photo-graphs the
spectator.[35]

In this formulation, the gaze is on the side of the object rather than the subject. Žižek illustrates his point by giving an example of a subject in a Hitchcock movie who approaches a threatening house: "The subject's eye sees the house, but the house—the object—seems somehow to return the Gaze."[36] Or, as Lacan himself states:

I can feel myself under the gaze of someone whose eyes
I do not see, not even discern. All that is necessary is for
something to signify to me that there may be others there.
This window, if it gets a bit dark, and if I have reasons for
thinking that there is someone behind it, is straight-away a
gaze.[37]

In this context, Žižek presents an account of suture that is slightly different from the one I've gleaned from Silverman.[38] Žižek's emphasis lies not on narcissistic identification or narrative resolution—which define suture for Silverman—but rather on the cinematic process that obscures the realization that "the show is run by the Absent One (or, rather, Other) who manipulates images behind my back"; suture, in this sense, is the cinematic operation by which "the threatening intrusion of the decentering Other, the Absent Cause" is neutralized.[39]

Žižek focuses on what is potentially unsettling (the recognition that an "Absent One" manipulates what I see) rather than on what is reassuring (narcissistic identification and narrative resolution) about movies. If Silverman stresses the ideological function of suture, the manner in which suture reinforces socially acceptable versions of (masculine and feminine) subjectivity, Žižek foregrounds the fact that the cinematic apparatus as a signifying system isn't a closed one but always, implicitly at least, refers to, yet also attempts to render invisible, what remains outside of it (the "Absent One"). Yet the result of the failure of suture in the Žižekian scenario is arguably the same as in the Silvermanian scenario: the spectator is no longer complacently engulfed by the narrative.

What is particularly instructive about Žižek's interpretation for our purposes is that he connects the collapse of the spectator's complacency, the intrusion of the "Absent One," to the Lacanian gaze: the house that looks back in the Hitchcock movie and the darkened window that Lacan refers to are disturbing because, like the sardine can, they appear to gaze at the viewer, thereby making it impossible for him or her to ignore the "Absent One" who manipulates the whole scene. This is because, as Žižek explains, there is no place in the cinematic frame for "the Gaze as the point from which the viewed object itself 'returns the Gaze' and regards us, the spectators."[40] The moment such a gaze appears, the moment the house or the window returns the viewer's look, the cinematic frame is broken, suture wavers, and the "Absent One," the wizard behind the curtain, is revealed.

This is why Žižek specifies that one of the biggest threats to suture is "a *point-of-view shot* which will not be clearly allocated as the point of view of some protagonist, and which will thus evoke the specter of a free-floating Gaze without a determinate subject to whom it belongs."[41] Hitchcock's house and Lacan's darkened window are sites of precisely such a free-floating gaze: a gaze that can't be attributed to a specific subject. Such a gaze is that of "an impossible subjectivity," which is why it can't be "found in the actuality of the spectator's experience."[42] This is a tangible way to understand McGowan's claim that the Lacanian gaze is a blank spot (a lack or absence) in our field of vision. Though we see the house or the window, we don't actually *see* its gaze (we only see it in our imagination). As Žižek concludes, "This gaze effectively *is* missing, its status being purely fantasmatic."[43]

The object that looks back refuses to remain an inert object, almost claims the status of a subject, with the result that the viewer's own subjective coherence, and certainly his or her ability to master the consumed images, is put in question. This is another way to grasp why, as I mentioned above, the Lacanian gaze appears to be the exact opposite of Mulvey's male gaze. This is why McGowan asserts that, from a Lacanian perspective, we should use the word "look" rather than "gaze" when talking about the subject's act of looking (the act that Mulvey analyzes).[44] On this view, even though Mulvey explicitly references Lacan, her reading of the male gaze is more Foucaultian than Lacanian, more focused on heteropatriarchal power—on the way that men dominate women—than on the decentering and traumatizing impact of the (desiring) subject's encounter with an image that seems to stare back.

Still, there may be points of compatibility between these divergent interpretations of the gaze. For starters, as I've indicated, the male gaze can be decentering and traumatizing for the woman who finds herself the object of this gaze. This woman may not be disoriented by her own desire. But she may be unsettled by her (often unwilled) encounter with the desire of the man looking at her. On the one hand, the male gaze certainly seems entirely different from the eerie gaze that Žižek describes in the sense that, unlike the latter, it can usually be attributed to a specific subject. On the other, *from the perspective of the woman who becomes its target*, it can take on precisely the same uncanny, disconcerting, and threatening quality that Žižek and other Lacanians associate with the Lacanian gaze.

Sometimes this is the case because the male gaze takes on an openly aggressive valence. But other times—and this is where the comparison to the Lacanian gaze becomes viable—it's because, just like I don't actually see the gaze of the house in Hitchcock's movie even though I'm aware of it, I often don't actually see the male gaze even though I'm acutely aware of it: I *know* that a man is looking at me but because I'm too disturbed (intimidated by his attention) to look back, I don't actually see him looking at me. But I sense his gaze all the same. In a way, I see his gaze without seeing it. Isn't this more or less what the Lacanian gaze—the gaze that is a blank spot in my field of vision—is all about? Isn't it an excellent example of what Lacan is talking about when he states, "I can feel myself under the gaze of someone whose eyes I do not see, not even discern"?

This scenario is most obvious in situations where I sense myself to be the object of the gaze of more than one man at a given moment, as can be the case when I'm passing a group of construction workers on the street. In such a situation, I can't locate the gaze even when I know that it's present; I may gain a glimpse of it by looking up briefly but then it becomes invisible to me because I instantly look away (because I know that returning the look would be likely to cause the scene to escalate from silent looking to verbal commentary, even heckling, of some kind). The same dynamic can also transpire in a situation where I intuit that I'm being looked at by just one man, say, on the subway, and I'm too timid (terrorized into submission) to look up and concretely discern his gaze (in a moment I'll return to what can happen if I do look up).

In both instances, I see the male gaze without seeing it. Indeed, insofar as I don't dare to look at it, I might as well be in one of Hitchcock's movies, confronted by an unnerving house. This is why, thinking both with and beyond the critics I've quoted, I'm tempted to assert that, from the perspective of the woman who is the target of the male gaze, the disconcerting and traumatizing quandary is the same as with the sardine can, the house, and the window: from the viewpoint of this woman, a man, particularly an unknown man, who looks at her, is an uncanny *object* that (against all logic) insists on looking at her (the subject).

Let me explain. As much as heteropatriarchy insists on defining the woman as an object, her experiential reality (usually) is that of a subject: in her *own* eyes, she (usually) is a subject, and this is the case even when she participates in her own objectification. Even a woman who is used to thinking of herself as an object of male desire presumably on some level also regards herself as a subject. From this it follows that, in relation to her—the subject of her story (the subject of the life she's leading, or stumbling through, when she's not busy trying to appear desirable)—a man, particularly an unknown man, who looks at her can come across as a vaguely threatening and often decidedly creepy object that, like the sardine can that refuses to (inconspicuously) blend into the ocean, refuses to remain an inanimate entity that (discreetly, benevolently) blends into the background of everyday life.

We've learned that the decentering and traumatizing aspect of the male gaze is that it attempts to turn a female subject into an object. But what adds a layer of uncanniness to the transaction is that it's orchestrated by an entity that, from my point of view, is an object. A strange man who looks at me is not a subject (to me). I know nothing about him. As far as I'm concerned, he could just as well be a sardine can. He remains an inert screen, a meaningless object. But when he looks at me—and particularly when he assesses me—he insists on being a subject. He insists on being meaningful (even when I have no time, space, or energy for his "meaning"). And he does so at the expense of my subjectivity. In the plus-minus game of heteropatriarchal gender relations, he reckons that he can only be an active subject, an entity with power, if he strips me of my subjectivity, if he turns me into a passive object. There is a violence in this transaction: in the same way as the gaze in the Lacanian sense threatens to shatter the subject's coherence, the male gaze in Mulvey's sense can threaten to shatter a woman's subjectivity.

There is a further parallel worth contemplating. Recall that McGowan maintains that the gaze in the Lacanian sense limits the subject's visual field. Well, the male gaze does exactly the same to me, albeit perhaps in a more concrete sense: when it compels me to look down or away, it causes me to miss everything that surrounds it, even things that I might very much like to see. This may in fact be one of its most brutal aspects. For instance, I might be looking at a beautiful vista of ocean, maybe even squinting to see if I can spot a sardine can in it, when a man cockily inserts himself into my field of vision, turns his eyes on me, and looks intently enough to force me to look away. I lose my ocean. This is hugely annoying. Alternatively, I might be reading a book on a park bench when I become aware of the male gaze, and suddenly the words no longer make any sense to me. This is also annoying. I really don't need to see the male gaze for it to rob me of half of my world precisely by limiting my visual field.

This is of course not how all women experience the male gaze. What I've presented here is the somewhat paranoid reading of a woman who attributes her chronic back pain to twenty-five years of being the daily target of the male gaze (and the bodily contortion caused by the attempt to deflect this gaze). Other women may welcome the male gaze as flattering (a point I'll emphasize in the second half of this chapter). But what I've offered as a potentially idiosyncratic scenario also seems to be the gist of Mulvey's theoretical formulation, which explains why I'm less willing than many of my fellow feminists to discard her account as pathetically outdated.

More relevantly, according to the logic of Mulvey's argument, the reverse of the scenario I've outlined is the trouble that begins for the male subject when the female object of his gaze looks back. In this situation, the tables are turned: the woman who in the eyes of the man should remain an object insists on being a subject; she becomes the uncannily animate object, a semi-subject (the house, the window) that gazes back, that refuses to settle into her role as a passive object, thereby (sometimes) flustering the male subject. As de Lauretis observes, whenever a woman actively looks, "castration is in the air."[45] I'll discuss this idea in greater detail below. For now, I merely want to note that if we shift our focus from the subject of Mulvey's male gaze to its object, an object that can sometimes decide to look back, we find ourselves in a territory that—potentially at least—is somewhat compatible with the more strictly Lacanian account of the gaze favored by Žižek and McGowan.

One might say that the gaze of any object—be this object a man, a woman, a person of some other gender, an inanimate entity, or Derrida's cat[46]—is always potentially decentering and traumatizing for the subject who thinks of itself as the rightful possessor of the gaze. From this viewpoint, the gender of the object that gazes back at the viewing subject doesn't matter: the object, whoever or whatever it is, steals the gaze that the subject believes should by default be its prerogative. However, what feminist theory adds to this otherwise seemingly neutral scenario is the component of heteropatriarchal power: the fact that men in our society have historically been more empowered than women, that they have historically been defined as active subjects rather than as passive objects, means that their gaze—the moment when the strange man who, for me, is a mere object turns his eyes upon me and insists on turning *me* into an object—can arguably cause more psychic havoc than the opposite scenario. (Incidentally, the same dynamic is easy to trace in racist situations, as Frantz Fanon famously does when he talks about being the black object of "the white gaze" in the Paris of the 1940s.[47])

The arguments I've just presented clarify why characters in mainstream movies, such as *Pretty Woman*, don't usually look back at the spectator. *The Good Wife*—a television show that sometimes strives to be daring—begins Season 6 with Alan Cumming staring at the viewer (almost) directly. The effect is not only uncanny; it also destroys suture in exactly the way I've described: the spectator is immediately aware of the cinematic apparatus that's manipulating images behind his or her back. This is why *Pretty Woman*'s Vivian can't look directly at the spectator. Doing so would instantly shatter the movie's fantasy world and destroy the viewer's investment in the narrative. Generally speaking, romantic comedies and other mainstream movies are much less likely to contain any version of the Lacanian gaze than more artistic movies, which often deliberately seek to disconcert and traumatize the viewer.

Voyeurism, fetishism, and the masquerade of femininity

Mulvey's depiction of the male gaze has thus undergone important challenges and revisions. Yet, as I've stressed, some of its elements remain relevant to contemporary film criticism. Indeed, I suspect that Mulvey's theory may be *more* relevant in the context of twenty-first-century media scholarship—which often focuses on lowbrow cultural products such as romantic comedies and television shows—than it was at the height of psychoanalytic feminist film theory of the 1980s. In other words, it may be that one reason Mulvey failed to convince many of her colleagues in psychoanalytic film theory (and even less the Lacanian critics of the 1990s and 2000s) is that the latter tended to study the high end of Hollywood (including Hitchcock), urbane European films, and erudite avant-garde productions—the kinds of sophisticated productions that make her theory seem overly simplistic.

Many of the criticisms leveled against Mulvey lose their power when we shift our attention from a film such as *Vertigo* to the average romantic comedy. Hitchcock may have been too smart to offer a straightforward depiction of the male gaze, choosing to foreground its violence instead. But contemporary romcoms dish out this gaze candidly, unhesitatingly, and unapologetically. And they routinely neutralize its misogynistic (decentering and potentially traumatizing) aspects. Consequently, it would be easy to assert that, unlike *Vertigo*, they do indeed teach women to take pleasure in their own sexual objectification.

I don't think that this is the *only* thing that romantic comedies do. As I noted in the Introduction—and as I'll illustrate in detail in the next chapter—even thoroughly mainstream movies, such as *Pretty Woman*, can contain progressive elements that undermine our culture's dominant codes of gender. This may in fact be what spectators find most compelling about them. This is to say that I'm not sure that suture is invariably a matter of viewers uncritically accepting familiar social roles. Sometimes we're riveted by narratives (or characterizations) that unravel such roles. This is why I believe that Hollywood movies aren't always merely a means of selling us the gendered status quo of our society but also frequently stretch the very parameters of this status quo.

This is one way in which social change takes place. Still, if one is going to look for a convincing case study for Mulvey's version of the male gaze, romantic comedies are a good place to start. This is why I want to round off the first half of this chapter by introducing three intertwined psychoanalytic concepts that Mulvey already analyzed and that are, in turn, related to the male gaze: voyeurism, fetishism, and the masquerade of femininity. These concepts will crop up at the end of my interpretation of *Pretty Woman* in the next chapter.

Of the three concepts at hand, voyeurism is perhaps the most intuitively accessible. Freud proposed that it's based on scopophilia: the pleasure of looking at other people. You can see how cinema—along with other visual media such as television and the internet—exploit our voyeuristic tendencies in the sense that a big part of the pleasure it provides is the thrill of being the unseen spectators of screen images. The darkness of the movie theater, like the privacy of the domestic spaces where images are most often consumed in today's society, explicitly places the spectator in the position of a voyeur (or Peeping Tom).

But voyeurism can also function within the movie narrative. Mulvey notes that classic Hollywood film explicitly displays female characters in ways that feed not only the voyeuristic fantasies of spectators but also those of the male protagonist. For instance, woman in classic cinema tends to function as an enigma to be "solved" by the male protagonist. This plot device allows the male gaze to linger on her unimpeded. In addition, the elusive woman is frequently destroyed (even killed) by the end of the movie. In this sense, the voyeuristic impulse easily slides into sadism, most commonly manifesting itself as an attempt to punish the woman for whatever it is that she's deemed to be hiding.

Vertigo renders this dynamic blatantly obvious, for it invites its spectators, as well as Scottie, to spy on Madeleine in an attempt to uncover her mystery. Indeed, as I noted earlier, the film's voyeurism is far from unconscious: Hitchcock foregrounds the conventions of voyeurism to the point of forcing spectators to confront the problematic nature of their pleasure in watching Madeleine through Scottie's eyes. Furthermore, Hitchcock underlines the aggression embedded in voyeurism by killing off Judy-as-Madeleine at the end. That this comes after Madeleine has already "died" twice within the movie narrative leaves no doubt of the fact that the idealized woman of the voyeuristic gaze must eventually be punished. Might this be because she has the power to elicit this gaze in the first place?

The second psychoanalytic concept that is related to the male gaze—one that is closely connected to voyeurism—is fetishism: the attempt to neutralize the threat that femininity as an embodiment of lack poses for the male spectator. To understand what I mean, it helps to refer back to Silverman's analysis of suture as what allows spectators to feel whole. What I didn't mention in the context of Silverman is that many feminist film critics have hypothesized that whenever a female character enters a film's visual space, she poses a potential problem for the male spectator for the simple reason that, as I've explained, woman in our culture signifies the prospect of castration; she personifies the very lack that suture is designed to conjure away. As Mulvey posits, the female figure on screen challenges the male spectator's coherence because she "connotes something that the look continually circles around but disavows: her lack of a penis, implying a threat of castration and hence unpleasure."[48]

This is the context in which we should understand de Lauretis's observation—quoted above—that whenever a woman on screen actively looks, "castration is in the air." It's how a woman becomes comparable to Hitchcock's eerie house or Lacan's darkened window. On the one hand, woman's "lack" provides the contrast that helps establish the male subject's phallic adequacy; on the other, the very presence of her body—on an unconscious level—reminds the male viewer of his potential inadequacy, of his potential castration, with the result that even when this body is displayed for his pleasure, it must simultaneously be contained. This is why, as de Lauretis succinctly puts it, "she must not look."[49]

According to this interpretation, mainstream cinema turns women into passive objects of the male gaze in order to neutralize the danger that an active female gaze would pose to male subjectivity as a site of phallic power; female objectification, in short, is a defense mechanism against the castration threat emanating from woman as a figure of lack. I think of this every time the following scene ensues in the Boston subway: I catch a man looking at me with an assessing gaze; due to my annoyance, I refuse to do the polite thing and look away; I become the house, the window; he reacts with belligerence, either by trying to stare me down or, less frequently, by calling me a "bitch."

Not coincidentally, this dynamic never takes place with men who are easily read as socially powerful: such men avert their gaze (presumably because they have nothing to lose). It's men whose social power is precarious—who are already too close to feeing castrated—who can't tolerate a woman's "castrating" (active) gaze. As women have long known, the most effective way to bypass this type of masculine aggression is to consent to staying the passive object of the male gaze; the solution is to look down, thereby temporarily extinguishing one's subjectivity. Yet doing so repeatedly can be psychologically eroding.

Feminist film critics have explored the mechanisms of fetishism in order to understand how mainstream cinema copes with the potentially disruptive presence of women on screen, starting from the premise that fetishism can take one of three forms: (1) a fixation on a specific erotic prop (such as a shoe); (2) a fixation on a specific detail of a woman's body (such as a lock of hair); or (3) a fixation on the entire female form as an incarnation of perfection (rather than of lack). In mainstream cinema, the third form is the most common.

Freud theorized fetishism as a glitch in (some) men's "normal" sexual functioning, arguing that men who are unable to overcome their castration fears are unable to attain sexual satisfaction with a woman without somehow being distracted from the fact that she doesn't have a penis.[50] The fetish object functions as such a distraction: the man becomes so focused on the props of femininity (shoes, lingerie, lipstick, false eyelashes, elaborate hair style, and so on) that his attention is diverted from the terrifying "wound" of female genitals. Alternatively, the whole woman is turned into a fetish, as Madeleine is in *Vertigo*. As Mulvey remarks, fetishism "builds up the physical beauty of the object, transforming it into something satisfying in itself."[51] Simply put, fetishism allows the male subject to disavow female "lack" even when he's on some level aware of it.

In this context, it might be prudent to remind ourselves that women don't, in reality, lack anything. Clearly, the equipment that women have is just as good as what men have. The point, again, is merely that heteropatriarchy has constructed women as lacking because they don't happen to have the organ that this system venerates (and replicates in its signifiers of power, such as its totem poles and, let's face it, the Washington Monument). Fetishism, in turn, represents heteropatriarchy's attempt to cope with the fact that women's so-called lack can remind men of the possibility that they could also become lacking. As I've explained, Lacan insists that they already *are* lacking. But this probably isn't what the average guy wants to hear. This guy will do anything in his power to banish the specter of castration. Fetishism is one way to accomplish this task. In the world of movies, as in the "real" world, fetishism transforms a potentially traumatizing female figure into a reassuring presence.

One could even say that femininity as a cultural construct is intrinsically a matter of fetishizing the female form, of finding ways to accentuate its pleasing characteristics and to downplay those deemed potentially offensive (because too "real"). The flipside of this is that fetishism seems in some ways to be built into the heteropatriarchal male psyche, so that many men are conditioned to enjoy the various disguises and artifices that women use to exaggerate their femininity: they may complain about how long it takes their girlfriend to get ready for a night out, but they're usually just as pleased with the (reassuringly feminine) result as Scottie is with the Madeleine that Judy manages to reconstruct for him. This is why fetishism is closely connected to another important concept in psychoanalytic feminist film theory: the masquerade of femininity.

This concept was invented by one of Freud's first female disciples, Joan Riviere. In her 1929 "Womanliness as a Masquerade," Riviere argued that women sometimes choose to wear an exaggerated version of femininity—an excess of femininity—as a mask to compensate for their usurpation of phallic power. I'll come back to Riviere's point about hyperbolic femininity in a moment. But first, let's pause at the idea that women can "usurp" phallic power. This is an idea that Lacan developed later when he argued that phallic power isn't intrinsically aligned with the possession of the penis. But Riviere already recognized that it was possible to detach phallic power from the penis, which meant that women could aspire to this power in various ways.

I like to think about the matter concretely, as a practice of picking up the "phallus"—an object or an attitude that, in our society, symbolizes power—when I'm about to enter a professional situation where a display of authority is needed. Queens need their capes, crowns, and specters. Likewise, female professionals walking into courtrooms, business meetings, operating rooms, or classrooms need various props. I know that I seize my metaphorical phallus whenever I step up to the podium of a large lecture hall. Sometimes I grip it so tightly that my knuckles go white. And sometimes . . . well, sometimes I drop it with a clang. If I've been teaching Lacan, I might even say, "Oops, I just dropped my phallus."

Due to the conceptual link that our society draws between the phallus and the penis, women have to work harder than men to convince the surrounding world that they're up to the task in situations where they're required to wield power; they have to find ways to overcome their coding as "lack." Worse still, women can be punished for exercising phallic power *too* effectively. This is where the masquerade of femininity comes in. According to Riviere, this masquerade is an attempt to counteract the punishment that might ensue from having usurped phallic power in ways that threaten masculine prerogative. More specifically, Riviere argues that professionally successful women, women who insist on their position as competent subjects (the position that heteropatriarchy reserves for men), resort to the masquerade of femininity in order to "hide the possession of masculinity and to avert the reprisals expected if she was found to possess it—much as a thief will turn out his pockets and ask to be searched to prove that he has not the stolen goods."[52]

Riviere here describes a defense mechanism that is familiar to many career women, namely the attempt to alleviate the sting of female achievement on the male ego by flamboyant displays of femininity, including flirtation. For women, adopting the mantle of power too convincingly can result in retaliation from men who feel cheated of their birthright and from other women who don't appreciate women who meddle with the established gender order. The masquerade of femininity seeks to offset such retaliation by reassuring others that the gender system hasn't been irreversibly altered, that the woman in question hasn't actually stolen masculinity (or masculine privilege) but remains a woman.

The masquerade of femininity could be said to differ from the normative construction of femininity—the process of becoming a woman that I've outlined—only in being more hyperbolic. This is why Riviere concludes that there is, in the final analysis, no discernible difference between being a woman in our society and the masquerade of femininity: "The reader may now ask how I define womanliness or where I draw the line between genuine womanliness and the masquerade. My suggestion is not, however, that there is any such difference; whether radical or superficial, they are the same thing."[53]

If femininity is a social role that little girls learn to perform early in their lives, the masquerade of femininity is merely an extravagant way of playing the game; it's a form of self-fetishization, except that in this instance the goal is to hide not the lack of a penis but its "illegitimate" possession.

Rise of third-wave feminism

In 1982, Mary Ann Doane elaborated on Riviere's notion of the masquerade of femininity in ways that, in hindsight, changed the face of feminist theory, including feminist film theory. Doane proposed that insofar as the masquerade of femininity foregrounds the artifice that goes into the construction of normative femininity, it creates a degree of distance between a woman and her image, thereby rendering this image *manipulable*. As Doane states, "The masquerade, in flaunting femininity, holds it at a distance. Womanliness is a mask which can be worn or removed."[54] If critics prior to Doane had emphasized the restrictive elements of normative femininity, Doane's articulation gave women an active role: they could choose to wear or remove the mask of womanliness at will, thereby gaining distance from, and control over, the very iconography of femininity that they were expected to embody.

If Western culture had traditionally mapped the male-female binary onto the mind-body binary in such a way that women were defined by bodily functions such as menstruation and childbearing, Doane's commentary on the masquerade of femininity placed the accent on art, skill, and style. According to her interpretation, women were not mere passive recipients of hegemonic definitions of femininity but could actively participate in the production of their femininity; the masquerade of femininity, in short, became a potential site of female agency. Doane could not have possibly known in 1982 that this insight was to become one of the founding concepts of third-wave feminism, for it took Judith Butler's *Gender Trouble* (1990) to fully draw out its theoretico-political implications.

Gender Trouble, which quickly became the bible of both third-wave feminism and queer theory, made many of the arguments about the fashioning of masculinity and femininity that I've already summarized.[55] However, what ushered Butler into prominence was her ability to convincingly demonstrate what Doane's articulation of the masquerade of femininity already gestured toward, namely that the performance of gender can become a scene of agency. More specifically, Butler illustrated that normative codes of gender can be turned against the very heteropatriarchal system of power that perpetuates them.

Butler argued that gender as a lived reality results from the repeated performance of preexisting blueprints of gendered comportment. This doesn't mean that we rifle through our closet every morning, deciding how we're going to "perform" our gender (though these days more and more people, in part thanks to Butler's analysis, are doing precisely this). Rather, as I've explained, the semiautomatic enactment of collective modalities of gendered behavior in time solidifies into a consistent gender identity. However, what most interests us—as it interested feminists of the 1990s—is Butler's claim that the performative nature of gender opens up the possibility of performing it transgressively.

Butler proposed that when we refuse to repeat dominant codes of gender faithfully, when we find various ways to "misrepeat" them, we throw a monkey wrench into our society's efforts to fix gender into a binaristic system that clearly separates men from women; we expose the artificial character of masculinity and femininity, thereby challenging the notion of natural sexual difference as well as the ideology of heteronormativity that this notion sustains. Over time, such defiance can incrementally alter the order of things: a misrepetition that is performed often enough, or insistently enough, can bring new forms of gendered behavior into existence.

In building her argument, Butler relied on Michel Foucault's theory of social power. In Foucault's view, power is not necessarily (or only) something that some people wield over others, as is the case, for instance, in a dictatorship. Rather, power, like the Lacanian symbolic order, is an invisible network of ideological conditioning that permeates the entire social fabric, reaching the deepest recesses of our being in ways that we can never fully account for.[56] This is the notion of power that I relied on earlier when I talked about femininity as a heteropatriarchal invention. What I want to add to the story now is the component of Foucault's theory that Butler capitalized on, namely that Foucault acknowledged that power is not infallible, that the hegemonic social order contains gaps, fissures, and points of vulnerability that can cause it to malfunction.

According to Foucault, power tends to create its own resistances so that, for example, an attempt to repress sexuality can generate a host of new sexual practices; when one pathway of sexual expression is cut off, people find ways to create new pathways, thereby giving rise to a whole new array of sexual possibilities. In this sense, every social restriction produces a set of unforeseeable possibilities; every tyranny produces a set of resistant forces. Power, in sum, is productive as well as restrictive, positive as well as negative.

This conception of power allowed Butler to assert that the misrepetition of dominant codes of gender, such as the parodies of gender offered by drag performances, can function as a resistant cultural practice. On the one hand, power in Foucault's terms is insidious in consisting of a nebulous network of social influences that are hard to attack because they don't converge at a clearly definable center; on the other, Foucault opened up a way of envisioning agency as what arises from the manipulation of dominant cultural ideologies. Third-wave feminism and queer theory, which both placed a strong accent on the constructedness of gender and sexuality, found this approach generative, with the result that the "performativity" of gender became a prominent theme in post-1990 American theory.

During the early years of third-wave feminist enthusiasm, it was difficult to perceive what in retrospect seems like a considerable problem with the Butlerian approach, which is that it relies on the very power that it seeks to subvert. After all, every "misrepetition" of gender presupposes—and in some ways reinforces—the hegemonic codes of gender it opposes. Take the performance of masculinity undertaken by butch lesbians. Undoubtedly, this performance reveals the socially constructed status of masculinity, thereby countering the naturalization of gender; it effectively dissociates masculinity from the biological male body. Yet to function successfully, it must draw on a readily identifiable pool of gender norms, so that on some level it merely replenishes this pool. The same is perhaps even more obviously the case with the masquerade of (straight) femininity as an overstatement of normative femininity.

This is why the political implications of contemporary displays of hyperfemininity—which I've linked to the resurgence of "girliness" in twenty-first-century American culture and which I'm about to discuss at greater length—remain unclear, with some critics lauding such displays as subversive and others viewing them as a continuation of heteropatriarchy. The matter is particularly charged because it's now easy to see what was less evident in the 1990s, namely that Butler's theory of gender performativity aligns fairly effortlessly with neoliberal, individualistic ideals of self-improvement and consumer capitalism. In finding ever new ways of performing its identity, the Butlerian subject exhibits some of the same characteristics as the neoliberal subject who seeks ever new editions of itself through consumerist attempts to cultivate its distinctive identity. As I'll demonstrate below, even the stylized performance of gender depends heavily on props made available by consumer culture.

Generally speaking, it's difficult to assess the political implications of the intellectual breakthroughs of the 1990s. Some of these breakthroughs were momentous, changing the way scholars approach fundamental questions regarding subjectivity, gender, power, and agency. Poststructuralist theory, which reached its apex at the same time as third-wave feminism, engaged in a relentless interrogation and deconstruction of stable identity categories, aligning political resistance with the destabilization of our understanding of the basic building blocks of human life. Likewise, third-wave feminists insisted that masculinity and femininity were supple categories that afforded a great deal of leeway for play. Among other things, if second-wave feminists had taken the definition of womanhood to be fairly obvious—and had seen feminism as a defense of the rights of this womanhood—third-wave feminists illustrated that this definition was always open to question.

These paradigm shifts were in many ways hugely productive. Yet something was arguably also lost in the process. For example, in comparison to the second-wave feminist insistence on the importance of large-scale social change, third-wave feminism's focus on gender performativity seems politically muted. In saying this, I don't mean that third-wave feminism had no political impact, for its ideals regarding the fluidity of gender and sexuality trickled down to mainstream culture, considerably altering the contours of this culture. At the same time, because third-wave feminism followed poststructuralist theory in valorizing both the mobility of meaning and the fragmentation of identity, it failed to mount a cohesive political program; it failed to make a loud enough demand for the drastically revamped (nonpatriarchal) society that second-wave feminists had dreamed of.

Equally regrettably, in attempting to distance itself from second-wave feminism, third-wave feminism managed to portray its predecessor as decidedly unsexy and uncool. On the one hand, there were good reasons for this distancing: second-wave feminism frequently relied on an essentialist rhetoric of gender and sexuality—a rhetoric that understood gender and sexuality to be bodily "givens" that needed no explanation—that contradicted the constructivist spirit of third-wave feminism. On the other, the third-wave feminist assault on second-wave feminism was at times so vehemently articulated that it was possible to get the impression that it was second-wave feminism, rather than heteropatriarchy, that oppressed women. In a cultural environment where young women were increasingly turning away from feminism, this more or less extinguished second-wave feminism, so that, in a sense, third-wave feminism inadvertently dug the grave of its predecessor.

In addition, in developing the notion that women could gain agency by actively manipulating the coordinates of femininity—and even by playing normative femininity to the hilt—third-wave feminism became a feminism on high heels. Even critics, such as Butler, who themselves had no interest in wearing high heels, appeared perfectly happy with the idea of other women doing so. Against this backdrop, second-wave feminism, with its advocacy of sensible shoes, came to seem terribly frumpy.

I don't mean to imply that there is something inherently terrible about high heels: I wear them myself. Rather, I want to call attention to the fact that if so many young women outside the academy these days reject feminism as being prudish and somehow just too damn earnest, it's in part because third-wave feminism—in attacking second-wave feminism as too puritanical—gave them the vocabulary with which to do so. Other cultural factors, such as the rise of neoliberalism, certainly contributed to the phenomenon. But it's ironic that third-wave feminism, through its celebration of gender performativity, participated in the escalation of commercialized forms of hyperfemininity; though it was not the intention of third-wave feminism to promote female sexual objectification, the two phenomena cannot be entirely dissociated.

I'll return to the problematic of female sexual objectification toward the end of this chapter, not the least because it offers one of the keys to understanding the appeal of romantic comedies such as *Pretty Woman*. But first I need to examine some of the cultural factors that, besides third-wave feminism, help explain the contemporary phenomenon of women swapping feminism for sexual self-objectification. This requires an investigation of themes that have been central to twenty-first-century feminist attempts to grapple with media genres such as romantic comedies and television shows: neoliberal capitalism, commercialism, dominant happiness narratives, and the advent of hyperfemininity as an emblem of power.

Neoliberal capitalism

In recent years, neoliberal capitalism has become a major concern for academic critics, including feminist media critics. Neoliberalism is a politico-cultural attitude that endorses free-market economics, celebrates efficient pragmatism, idealizes personal achievement, and promotes individualistic solutions to collective social problems. Even though Foucault's musings on the topic predate the 1990s, when neoliberalism matured into a dominant creed in the United States, he captured the gist of its ethos when he argued that in the Western capitalist world, we've come to think of the individual as a miniature economic enterprise—what he called *homo economicus*—and of human life as a process of perfecting the functioning of this enterprise through various projects of self-development.[57]

Foucault made this argument in the context of explaining another concept that has become popular with twenty-first-century critics: "biopolitics" as an invisible politics of life (of *bios*) that fashions us as human beings in fundamental ways, penetrating the most minute details of existence. In many ways, biopolitics is simply another name for social power, for the clandestine network of ideological manipulation that I discussed earlier in the context of gender socialization. However, in his analysis of biopolitics, Foucault paid particular attention to how the market mentality characteristic of capitalist economies has, in neoliberal societies, such as contemporary American society, been applied to the individual, so that people have started to conceptualize their lives in terms of smart investments, optimum performance, and increased productivity.

Consider, for instance, the manner in which many of us take it for granted that our investment in education—the accumulation of cultural capital—will yield a benefit in terms of future performance and productivity, allowing us to make a better living (make a profit, as it were). For many Americans, this way of thinking is so commonsensical that it can be difficult to recognize that there may be other equally valid ways of organizing our lives. Perhaps there are goals other than making a good living—such as the cultivation of relationships, friendships, and communities—that could be considered more important. Americans do value these things as well, you might respond, and you would be right. But you would have to admit that, for many Americans, these things, ideally at least, *presuppose* the ability to make a decent living. And you would also have to admit that many Americans believe that the cultivation of good relationships, friendships, and communities begins with the self—with the self's ability to manage all components of its life to its satisfaction.

The cornerstone of neoliberal capitalist ideology is the notion that effort will lead to success, that hard work and striving will be rewarded. This notion was already the linchpin of the American dream, which is perhaps one reason that neoliberal capitalism has thrived in the United States more than in other parts of the Western world, which sometimes still cling to the rudiments of the social welfare state (such as socialized medicine). It's not for nothing that one of the most persistent components of American cultural mythology is that Americans are a robust people, capable of bouncing back from any setback or obstacle. As a matter of fact, it's almost as if attaining the good life that the American dream promises doesn't even really count unless it's preceded by some struggle. The ability to triumph on the basis of talent, exertion, and perseverance has always been the centerpiece of this dream. Neoliberal capitalism has merely bolstered this mentality.

The insidious underside of this neoliberal creed is the often unstated but pervasive belief that if someone hasn't managed to attain the good life (meaning, first and foremost, a good living), it must be because she hasn't tried hard enough. Maybe she's just lazy, willing to live off unemployment benefits.

Or maybe there is something wrong with her: maybe she's mentally unstable. Or maybe she's haunted by some personal tragedy. In the latter case, she gets some sympathy. But ultimately she really should be able to snap out of it; she should be able to slay her inner demons so as to become a productive member of society. Within this performance-oriented mentality, even prolonged sadness is a problem because it makes you unproductive. When someone close to you dies or abandons you, you're allowed to grieve for a while but the kind of grief that doesn't come to a timely end is considered self-indulgent—a weakness of character. You're supposed to pull yourselves up by your bootstraps, dust yourself off, and get back into the fray of making a living (and spending it).

What gets brushed under the rug in this vision are the structural impediments—such as sexism, racism, homophobia, and economic disparities—that keep some people from thriving no matter how hard they try. When it comes to gender, for instance, neoliberal capitalism wants us to believe that because men and women are now legally entitled to the same opportunities, the only thing that's holding women back is their lack of effort (or aptitude). After all, if a woman can be the secretary of state or the attorney general, what's keeping you from rising to the top of the career ladder? Might it be your bad attitude that's holding you back?

Think of Uncle John rolling his eyes at the dinner table when you complain about a sexist image you saw on television. He doesn't want to hear about it. It ruins his perfectly good day. So you're told to "get over" it because there is no point to pondering such matters, given that there is nothing you can do about them anyway; you're told to channel your energies into something more useful, such as your personal goals (surely *you* aren't going to be held back by sexist discrimination? surely *you* won't let yourself be defeated in that way?). Essentially, you're told to keep your complaints to yourself so that you don't poison everyone else's life.

You can see how neoliberalism easily leads to postfeminism: the conviction that men and women are already so equal that feminism is no longer necessary, that it might in fact be the enemy of female empowerment because it propagates defeatist messages about gender inequality that threaten to undermine women's confidence in their ability to compete in the professional realm. You can also see how contemporary media culture participates in this mentality. As Susan Douglas points out in *The Rise of Enlightened Sexism* (2010), the continuous parade of tough action heroines and savvy female professionals in today's movies and television shows generates fantasies of equality that cover over social realities of persistent inequality.

How many black female judges are there in the real world? If television shows are to be believed, being black and female is one of the prerequisites for becoming a judge. In this way, media fantasies obscure the fact that black women still find it disproportionately difficult to enter prestigious professions, and that women, generally speaking, still earn less than men do on average. In the next chapter, I'll argue that many of us are able to retain a degree of critical distance from the media images we consume. Still, Douglas is right to suggest that media portrayals that communicate that women have made it—and that feminism is therefore obsolete—can mask "how much still remains to be done."[58]

In this context, recall that the 1990s, the decade during which both neoliberalism and postfeminism became consolidated as central components of American culture, is also the decade that witnessed the emergence of the romantic comedy as a new type of "girly" film. This isn't a coincidence. One reason feminist film critics have recently become so interested in neoliberalism as a culture of ambition and striving is that they've recognized that post-*Pretty Woman* romcoms consistently present the neoliberal success story as a desirable story of female development.

The female go-getter—the young women trying to beat the odds of career obstacles (often represented by other women who are scheming to block her success)—is integral to the plot lines of romcoms such as *Legally Blonde* (2001), *The Devil Wears Prada* (2006), and *Pitch Perfect* (2012). This figure of the female go-getter has also become popular in television shows (think of all the female lawyers, doctors, detectives, and fashion designers on television). My point is not that female professional success is deplorable—better this than Pamela Anderson running on a California beach with a surfboard, right?—but merely that the repetition of the trope of the struggling career woman who ultimately always beats the odds supports the neoliberal notion that it's up to the individual to succeed through relentless exertion.

Seeing powerful female role models in the media is reassuring. But the downside is that it can give us the impression that structural impediments have been overcome, that those who are still lagging behind are to blame for their lack of accomplishment, and that the only thing keeping me from becoming America's Next Top Model is that I haven't yet learned how to camouflage my physical flaws (but Tyra Banks can teach me). Or if that's unrealistic—I'm too old and short, after all—then at least I should be able to land a million-dollar book deal, buy a condo in Manhattan, rent a summer house on Martha's Vineyard, and drive a sleek Lexus in between. Isn't that what the combo of brains and hard work is supposed to get me? So what's wrong with me?

The promise of happiness

In neoliberal culture every problem has a practical solution: we just need to keep our chin up and find it. In this manner, the creed of efficient pragmatism meets the creed of cheerfulness. As Barbara Ehrenreich demonstrates in *Bright-Sided* (2009), in optimistic America, the creed of cheerfulness can be taken to such extremes that many people believe that the power of positive thinking alone can make them rich, bring them love, or cure them of cancer.[59] Related creeds—what feminist philosopher Sara Ahmed calls "happiness scripts"—include the conviction that love can heal all wounds, that marriage is the pinnacle of happiness, and that a loving family can compensate for all the wrongs of the world.[60] Note, once again, the individualistic nature of these aspirations: happiness results from fulfilling personal aspirations, including the aspiration to create happy marriages and families, rather than from collective attempts to alleviate social ills.

Ahmed proposes that dominant happiness scripts teach us to pursue a limited set of goals, ideals, and ambitions with a degree of automatism; because we believe that certain things (goals, ideals, and ambitions) will make us happy, we chase them even when we're extremely unlikely to attain them or even when they're unlikely to actually bring us the happiness we're after. Indeed, our commitment to dominant happiness scripts can be so strong that even when a given script doesn't deliver what it promises, when it makes us unhappy rather than happy, we don't think of questioning the script itself but instead assume that somehow we've failed to live it out correctly. Sometimes we don't even confess to being unhappy because we believe that if we just keep at it, if we just try hard enough, our preferred script will eventually usher us to the threshold of happiness.

Queer theorist Lauren Berlant has coined an apt term for this predicament: "cruel optimism." Berlant defines cruel optimism as the irrational belief that modes of life that hurt us will in the end grant us the good life, specifying that "a relation of cruel optimism exists when something you desire is actually an obstacle to your flourishing."[61] We hope against hope that our luck will change (soon, right?) even when it shows no sign of doing so. Even when we've never experienced the happiness we pursue, we tend to believe that attaining it is just a matter of time, that it's waiting for us around the corner. This is how we can end up endorsing forms of life that are not in the least bit good for us, coming, as Berlant claims, to "misrecognize the bad life as a good one."[62]

The happiness script that is among those most likely to mislead us in this way—and one particularly relevant to romantic comedies—is the marriage script. The message that meets us from movies, television, magazines, self-help books, and well-meaning relatives alike is that without marriage, our lives lack meaning, that marriage is an essential ingredient of the happy life. This message is so relentless that it can give the impression that even a toxic marriage—a marriage composed of boredom, frustration, aggression, and lackluster sex lives—is better than not being married; it can give the impression that if we opt out of marriage, we opt out of the very possibility of happiness.

Against this glorification of marriage, romantic relationships that don't lead to the altar can seem like mistakes. Indeed, from the perspective of the neoliberal creed that wants practical results for all of our exertions, they're mainly a waste of time. In this manner, the ethos of efficient pragmatism manages to infiltrate even our intimate lives. This pragmatism favors security over passion, viewing longevity as the hallmark of "real" love, so that a relationship that endures is considered a success even when it's largely uninspiring whereas one that doesn't last is considered a failure regardless of how vitalizing it might have felt. This in turn causes some people to work on their ailing relationships to an almost absurd degree, to stage heroic attempts to salvage alliances that are obviously past their expiration date. And because our culture—arguably rather naïvely—believes that the stability of marriages ensures the stability of our social order, it strives to make such labor-intensive intimacy, the ideal of "working for love," sound admirable, as the mature approach to relationships.

The persistence of gender stereotyping

Because most people in our society take it for granted that happiness is a worthy goal, the cultural portraiture of happiness that surrounds us is one of the most powerful (biopolitical) influences in our lives, dictating which life directions we choose to pursue and which to avoid. This portraiture of happiness remains deeply gendered, so much so that neoliberal culture often seems like a deliberate backlash against feminism: it enthusiastically endorses some of the very gender stereotypes that feminists worked so hard to dismantle.

When outlining Lacanian theory, I already mentioned that our society promotes the notion that men and women complement each other, which is one way in which it arrives at the conviction that heterosexual marriage represents the "natural" culmination of romance. But our society's Mars-Venus mentality reaches beyond the marriage script, implying that more or less every dimension of human subjectivity is dictated by the shape of our genitals. It advances the notion that men and women live in two very different sexual, emotional, and psychological universes.

The clichés about gender are as well-known as they're well-circulated: while men (supposedly) are aggressive, women (supposedly) are nurturing; while men are autonomous, women are relational; while men need space, women need intimacy; while men like sports, women like to cuddle; while men are willing to have sex with a telephone pole, women—at least the good kind—are sexually reluctant; while men are attracted by youth, beauty, and feminine vulnerability, women are looking for men with power, status, and financial resources; while men are promiscuous, women are the faithful sex; while men are aroused by porn, women need a lengthy courtship—flowers, conversation, expensive dinners, and flashy displays of devotion—to feel the slightest quiver of the needle.[63]

What's more, cultural authorities such as popular scientists and self-help authors try to convince us that most of our relationship problems arise from our inability to cross the gender divide. They leave little room for the possibility that couples might run into problems for the simple reason that romantic partners bring their unique personal experiences, unconscious motivations, existential struggles, histories of suffering, and points of vulnerability to the intimate encounter. Gender—and gender *alone*—is thought to be the cause of relationship troubles. And though there are occasional nods toward the idea that "some" men and women might deviate from dominant gender scripts, the overall assumption seems to be that the differences between them are self-evident and immutable.

It's of course not the case that everyone in our society buys such gendered reasoning. Rather, the problem is that it prevails in places—such as science—where it can do a great deal of damage. In 2013, the *New York Times* reported that since 2000, scientific journals have published more than 30,000 articles on the differences between men and women;[64] neuroscientists are tracking variations in male and female brain functioning; and education experts are devising differentiated learning strategies for boys and girls based on the idea that they have contrasting strengths (e.g., boys excelling in mathematical tasks and girls excelling in verbal tasks).

What is doubly bizarre about this practice of gender stereotyping is that it's done entirely matter-of-factly in a society that has otherwise gotten increasingly careful about the generalizations it makes about people based on group identities. For example, although racism continues to be a tremendous problem in today's society, it's not widely acceptable to cast judgment on people based on race alone, at least not among scientists and other academics (the Donald Trumps of the world may be a different story). But when it comes to gender, our cultural authorities, including some scientists and academics, are falling over each other to insist on the validity of the most outrageous stereotypes conceivable.

Here one must ask a version of the question that Freud already asked: why aren't women screaming bloody hell? Women tend to get the short stick of gender stereotyping. So why aren't they protesting more? It's difficult to find a black person who eagerly endorses our society's stereotypes about black people. But it's not at all hard to find a woman—of any color—who does exactly this regarding gender stereotypes (incidentally, it's also much easier to find a woman who ridicules feminism than it is to find a black person who ridicules the civil rights movement). Why is this? The reason I'll discuss in the rest of this chapter is that many women find the stereotypes of femininity satisfying: as I've suggested all along, women have been taught to take pleasure in normative femininity even when this femininity casts them in a subordinate position. But first, let me outline some less complicated reasons.

Foremost among these is that many straight women believe that learning to decipher the so-called "male psyche" will deliver them to the gates of romantic fulfillment. Inasmuch as they agree with self-help authors that relationship problems result from the misunderstandings of gender, they trust that figuring out what makes guys tick will instantly solve these problems. Even women who don't recognize themselves in the female stereotypes that our society holds up to them can be convinced that there is a grain of truth to the stereotypes of masculinity, so that these seem to offer a quick fix for the ambiguities of relating. That this is faulty reasoning becomes obvious when one admits that gay and lesbian couples are just as likely to have relationship problems as straight couples, so that it can't possibly be that gender differences are their primary cause. Yet straight women—who often feel responsible for making intimate relationships work—can be baited by the promise of definitive solutions to the tangles of relating.

Perhaps even more insidiously, cultural authorities who promote gender stereotypes are extremely good at implying that deviating from traditional femininity will result in the lack of love. Even self-help authors who are nominally trying to help women routinely suggest that any woman who refuses to abide by normative femininity—who is, say, too ambitious or self-sufficient—risks losing her man; the punishment for not performing one's gender correctly is misery, loneliness, and desolation. Our gender stereotypers have thus figured out that the best way to flood women with antifeminist ideas is to make them feel insecure about their basic desirability. This is why I think that dominant codes of romantic behavior—along with economic disparity—are among the strongest bastions of heteropatriarchy in our society, that they are a means of feeding otherwise confident women a hefty dose of submissiveness when their defenses are down.[65]

Gender stereotyping can also be a fairly transparent attempt to reconcile women to hurtful male behavior. Take the common notion that men are hardwired to cheat on women. The minute cultural authorities start claiming—as many of them do—that this is a scientifically proven fact, it becomes the perfect excuse for men to step out on their partners. It's in men's genes, so the poor sops can't help themselves. This in turn means that they can't be held responsible for it.

Unfortunately, when women believe that men's propensity to stray is intrinsic to their biological makeup, there isn't much they can do about it besides resigning themselves to their sorry lot, maybe crying a little, and eating a pint of Chunky Monkey. Note that I'm not saying that men are inherently faithful. It seems to me that many people—men and women alike—are prone to promiscuity. My point is rather that the *gendering* of promiscuity—the idea that it's a specifically masculine predilection—puts extreme pressure on women to be forgiving about male sexual behavior that they may experience as devastating. Likewise with other "masculine" lapses, such as commitment phobia, emotional incompetence, and amnesia about anniversaries: women are supposed to cut men slack because . . . well, they're *guys* so they can't be expected to be good at these things. This type of thinking serves the interests of heteropatriarchal men who are likely to mistreat women for the simple reason that they think that they have the right to do so.

On the flipside, those invested in gender stereotyping attempt to console women by reassuring them that they're good at all the things that our society has traditionally *devalued*: emotions, empathy, compassion, altruism, intuition, and nurturing. I'm not saying that it's bad to be good at these things—not at all. But these traits have throughout the ages been used to justify the idea that women's place is in the home, taking care of the young, smoothing over ruffled feathers, propping up male egos, and generally speaking, making sure that relationships survive.

So it's a little suspicious that, in the postfeminist era, women are once again supposed to claim them as "feminine" virtues. Let me put it this way: telling women that they're better than men at emotional intelligence may seem like a compliment, but it's also an invitation to work harder than men do at resolving emotional conflicts.

The new girliness

Against the backdrop of our culture's gender stereotyping practices, movies and television shows aimed at female audiences offer an interesting terrain of study, for they tend to resist many components of gender stereotyping—sometimes even deliberately breaking the molds of gender that this stereotyping promotes—at the same time as they insist that women must remain recognizably feminine. In the next chapter, we'll see that *Pretty Woman*'s ability to play both sides of this dynamic is among the attributes that contributed to its success. But first let me outline some of the ways in which recent feminist media scholarship—scholarship published well after *Pretty Woman*—has analyzed this phenomenon. How do female-centered movie and television narratives cope with contemporary culture's confusing jumble of antifeminist and feminist messages?

Such narratives tend to be ahead of the general cultural curve in the sense that, as opposed to those who promote the notion of immutable gender differences, they frequently make a point of portraying men and women as sharing fundamental characteristics: today's movies and television shows of the romcom genre showcase female characters who are just as likely to be driven and competent as male characters are; and, conversely, they present men who are just as likely to be emotionally open and vulnerable as women are. In sum, when it comes to psychological traits, career success, personal values, and general attitude toward life, men and women are depicted to be fairly similar.

However, this convergence of gender roles tends to be compensated for by a resolute celebration of femininity as a physical attribute. As Douglas complains, women can now "be legally equal but they had better be visually feminine": "it is precisely because women no longer have to exhibit traditionally 'feminine' *personality* traits—like being passive, helpless, docile, overly emotional, dumb, and deferential to men—that they must exhibit hyperfeminine *physical* traits—large boobs and cleavage, short skirts, pouty lips—and the proper logos linking this femininity to upper-class ranking."[66]

In *Neo-Feminist Cinema* (2011), Hilary Radner analyzes the rise of what she calls "the girly film": a film that constructs female subjectivity as a complex blend of career aspirations, spirited independence, sexual freedom, and "girly" hyperfemininity. Through this distinctive portraiture of female subjectivity, the girly film—which most romcoms could be said to be—stages an anxious encounter with our culture's conflicting messages regarding gender and gender equality. On the one hand, it doesn't want to give up on the privileges won by second-wave feminism; it doesn't want to backpedal on social, political, and economic equality. Nor does it want to return to older ideals of female sexual modesty. But, on the other hand, it seeks to alleviate cultural concerns about the possibility that men and women might end up being *too* similar by staging visual displays of hyperbolic femininity (or "girliness").

Radner remarks that girliness as a contemporary feminine ideal transcends age so that even middle-aged women—such as the perky characters of *Sex and the City: The Movie* (2008)— are expected to emulate it. As an attitude, it consists of a mixture of sassiness, playfulness, narcissism, and hedonism. As a "look," it's accomplished through fashion, shopping, consumer savvy, and voluntary self-objectification.

In relation to the larger cultural trends I've delineated, girliness can be situated at the intersection of neoliberalism and postfeminism. As Rosalind Gill and Christian Scharff posit, "The autonomous, calculating, self-regulating subject of neoliberalism bears a strong resemblance to the active, freely choosing, self-reinventing subject of postfeminism."[67] In addition, the girly subject is fashioned through an avid participation in consumer culture. From a cynical perspective, one might say that second-wave feminist ideals of liberation have been co-opted by the consumer fantasies of neoliberal capitalism to such an extent that, for many women today, to be "free" means being free to purchase everything that a decent department store makes available.

Along closely related lines, being "free" means being free to flaunt femininity— including hypersexualized femininity— without (supposedly) compromising on female emancipation. As Douglas wryly remarks, "By 1997 and 1998, the new girliness was everywhere, and it offered a fleeting fantasy that girls could have it both ways: they could be sex objects in fuck-me pumps and microminis while simultaneously critiquing patriarchal ways of looking at and thinking about young women."[68] The ideal of girliness, then, encapsulates the postfeminist dilemma of wanting to have it both ways, of wanting to be both feminine and equal. This dilemma is precisely why postfeminism, often opportunistically, appropriates second-wave feminist victories while at the same time rejecting feminism as too grim, dowdy, bitter, and belligerent—as the arch enemy of femininity.

As I've stressed, in many ways the combination of femininity and equality that postfeminism aspires toward is compatible with third-wave feminism. However, there is one enormous difference, and this is that third-wave feminists rarely endorse neoliberal capitalism and consumerism in the manner that postfeminism does. Even so, there are scholars, such as Radner, who have a degree of sympathy for the postfeminist sensibility, seeing it as a legitimate reaction to second-wave feminism's inability to address the concerns of women "who sought to preserve their identity as 'feminine' while aspiring to the kind of material comforts and achievements that define success in terms of neoliberalism."[69]

According to Radner, unlike feminism, postfeminism—or what she prefers to call "neofeminism" so as to better align it with neoliberalism—allows women to enhance "glamor as the sign of a new and revitalized feminine identity."[70] Neofeminism, Radner approvingly remarks, deals with matters concerning gender equality in a tone that is "less urgent and threatening" than that of feminism, therefore offering "an apparently safe environment that does not alienate the still dominant class of heterosexual men."[71] Using such male-friendly neofeminism as a model for what feminism, in general, should aspire to become, Radner advocates a facelift for feminism because, in her assessment, a feminism "that does not situate femininity as one dimension of the play of gender and identity within the broad terrain of neo-liberalism will continue to fail in its desire to make itself over in response to the new millennium."[72]

I find this conclusion problematic. I don't think that feminism should actively seek to insert itself into the individualistic and competitive terrain of neoliberalism: a system that notoriously relies on the exploitation of non-Western labor to ensure the availability of affordable consumer items in Western stores. Nor do I think that it's the task of feminism to provide a safe, non-alienating environment for (nonfeminist) straight men. Though I've emphasized that third-wave feminism views men as allies in the fashioning of a more egalitarian society, I draw a line at trying to appease masculine anxieties about the wobbly foundations of heteropatriarchy.

But perhaps most fundamentally, why should feminism try to accommodate women who explicitly reject it? Feminism, after all, is a political movement with a political agenda rather than a social club for women. Saying that feminism should embrace women who intentionally mock it is a bit like saying that antiracists should cater to the needs of white supremacists. Isn't it a bit unreasonable to demand that feminism speak to all women regardless of how antifeminist their views are?

I'm more inclined to agree with Douglas, who proposes that postfeminism is merely the latest edition of heteropatriarchy: one of the deceptive disguises that heteropatriarchy dons in neoliberal society. Douglas maintains that postfeminism facilitates a form of "enlightened sexism": a subtle and stealthy sexism that's better at hiding its inegalitarian underpinnings than older versions of patriarchy. According to Douglas, enlightened sexism is at bottom nothing but "good, old-fashioned, grade-A sexism that reinforces good, old-fashioned, grade-A patriarchy. It's just much better disguised, in seductive Manolo Blahniks and an Ipex bra."[73] In other words, though postfeminism certainly contains elements of embedded feminism, it also promotes the notion that, *precisely because feminist goals have (supposedly) been achieved*, "it's okay, even amusing, to resurrect sexist stereotypes."[74]

Douglas therefore suggests that enlightened sexism disseminates the message that because women are now equal, we're free to embrace things that used to be considered sexist, such as hypersexualized femininity, adding that enlightened sexism is frequently accompanied by a "knowing wink": "Guys are so dumb, such helpless slaves to big breasts, and the female display is, in the end, so harmless, that a feminist critique is not necessary. Therefore, the objectification of women is now fine; why, it's actually a joke on the guys. It's silly to be sexist; therefore, it's funny to be sexist."[75] In such a gendered universe, the extremeness of sexism proves that there is no sexism; its ironic, self-reflexive tone implies that it's not to be taken seriously, that it's all tongue-in-cheek. This is how postfeminism manages to make heteropatriarchy pleasurable for women by convincing them that their empowerment lies in sexual self-objectification.

Power femininity?

Postfeminism, like the romantic comedies that it has spawned, is characterized by a mixture of antifeminist and feminist ideals. Yael Sherman offers a helpful analysis of this predicament by distinguishing between traditional forms of femininity and what she calls "neoliberal femininity"—the kind of postfeminist femininity I've been discussing—in an attempt to explain why so many women find the latter compelling. According to Sherman, neoliberal femininity is attractive to women because instead of signaling passivity and submission, as traditional femininity did, it signals activity and autonomy.

Sherman notes that while traditional femininity connoted dependence, neoliberal femininity connotes independence; while traditional femininity was associated with vanity, neoliberal femininity is associated with the idea that one is actively self-responsible, able to take care of oneself like any good neoliberal subject; while traditional femininity sought to flatter men, neoliberal femininity announces women's intention to compete in both the public and private spheres as men's equal; and perhaps most significantly for our purposes, while traditional femininity cast women into the role of passive sex objects, neoliberal femininity implies active, competent subjectivity, including sexual autonomy. Traditional femininity was primarily a way for women to increase their value on the marriage market during an earlier era when they didn't yet have the option of supporting themselves through their own labor; it was, as Sherman puts it, "a tool of the weak,"[76] a tool the less powerful used to manipulate, through cunning, the more powerful. In contrast, neoliberal femininity—including its emphasis on sexual self-objectification—is wielded by today's women as a weapon of power.

Sherman acknowledges that neoliberal femininity contains elements of feminism (which she, like Radner, seems to equate with second-wave feminism). At the end, however, she reaches the conclusion toward which I'm also leaning, namely that this new femininity offers an illusion of power rather than genuine empowerment: "Neoliberal femininity may seem vaguely feminist—what's wrong with promoting self-confidence, happiness, and success?—but it is, at heart, an antifeminist ideal, based on disregarding structural inequality and embracing competition as the solution to all problems."[77]

Sherman uses *Miss Congeniality* (2000) to illustrate her point. This movie, like so many postfeminist media products, wants to have both (neoliberal, girly) femininity and equality. The first half of the movie, which gives us the hardboiled, not-in-the-least-bit-girly FBI agent Gracie Hart (Sandra Bullock), stages a critique of normative femininity and the male gaze, for Gracie caters to neither. The second half, however, withdraws this critique, showing us how Gracie, through her participation (as an undercover agent) in the Miss America pageant, comes to appreciate the pleasures of femininity, going as far as to explicitly retract her earlier snide comments on the Neanderthal mentality that causes women to participate in beauty pageants. Predictably, this is when her attractive coagent, Eric (Benjamin Pratt), starts to pay attention to her as a woman worth looking at: it's the elaborate makeover—replete with facials, tweaking, waxing, hair styling, and makeup, along with a new, skintight wardrobe—that Gracie undergoes for the sake of her undercover mission that activates the male gaze in the movie, so that post-makeover, Gracie becomes an object of Eric's desire.

That Gracie learns to value femininity may not be a problem per se, for as I've stressed, the denigration of femininity can be a patriarchal practice—one that implies that there is something inherently stupid and incompetent about feminine women. However, as Sherman argues, what is dubious about the plot of *Miss Congeniality* is that Gracie gains absolutely everything through her conversion to femininity: she solves the FBI case, saves the beauty pageant contestants, wins her man, and is crowned Miss Congeniality. Pre-femininity, Gracie is miserable, botching an undercover operation, punching a boxing bag, and heating up TV dinners in an ancient microwave that needs a beating to work; post-femininity, Gracie is happy at love and work alike.

Sherman is therefore right to point out that, when it comes to femininity, the movie is a bit schizophrenic: on the one hand, it offers an ironic take on the masquerade of femininity, showcasing the ridiculous amount of labor that goes into producing the polished feminine persona; Gracie's makeover is nothing but pleasurable. On the other, it implies that this effort is worth it by illustrating that femininity is what ultimately makes Gracie a more complete person—one able to balance romance with a demanding career. Femininity, in short, gives Gracie the grace that her name implies she should have but, at the beginning of the movie, clearly doesn't.

Notably, femininity is also what rescues Gracie from her lack of sexual confidence. As Sherman observes, as long as Gracie shuns femininity, she's neither sexual subject nor object, existing in a kind of erotic limbo. In contrast, her acquiescence to femininity turns her not just into a sexual object, the object of Eric's desire, but also—as is fitting for a modern liberated woman—into a sexual agent, capable of actively claiming the man she wants: at the end of the movie, she initiates the all-important kiss.

This is a powerful lesson: become feminine and you'll be loved. And you'll gain sexual confidence to boot. As enjoyable as *Miss Congeniality* is—and it is hugely enjoyable—its overall message is that the rejection of normative femininity simply just doesn't work for women, that the only way to succeed, even professionally, is to accept the codes of neoliberal femininity. It's perhaps then not surprising that the movie, despite its genuinely feminist elements, in the end portrays feminism—in Sherman's words—as "actively harmful" to women, as perhaps even "more oppressive than patriarchy."[78]

The surveillance gaze

While Radner asks feminism to accommodate neoliberal femininity, Sherman, like Douglas, suggests that neoliberal femininity is the undoing of feminism. However, all three critics agree that media portrayals of neoliberal femininity (or girly femininity) express a vision of female empowerment that is designed to be palatable to general audiences: this is female empowerment stripped of its feminist bite, friendly to both heteropatriarchy and consumerism.

Interestingly, while portrayals of neoliberal femininity usually attempt to conceal their complicity with heteropatriarchy, they have few qualms about being explicitly supportive of consumerism: the trope of girliness—celebrated not just by movies such a *Miss Congeniality* but by television shows such as *Sex and the City* (1998–2004), *Gossip Girl* (2007–12), and *Pretty Little Liars* (2010–)—blends harmoniously with conspicuous consumption. Girliness, after all, is first and foremost defined in terms of physical appearance, which, in turn, can be manipulated almost endlessly through the tools offered by consumer culture: from clothes, shoes, belts, and designer handbags to manicures, highlights, makeup, and cosmetic surgery, consumer culture provides ways to take the masquerade of femininity to a whole new level.

I've noted that neoliberalism values the ideal of self-improvement. In the case of women, this ideal frequently takes the form of endless attempts to render the body more appealing. Indeed, because the body is always intrinsically imperfect, there is in principle no limit to the "improvement" it can undergo, with the result that the female body becomes a site of intense intervention, constraint, regulation, and management.

In this sense, there is perhaps no better example of Foucault's notion of biopolitical control than the (youngish) female body, which is subjected to an unbelievable amount of discipline and punishment. Older women are of course not immune to this regimen either, often despairing at the impossibility of the task (while still doing their best to fit into skinny jeans). But it's young women in particular who are caught up in a vicious cycle of shopping, dieting, and monitoring every aspect of their physical being.

Within this mentality, no obstacle is insurmountable, no imperfection is beyond repair. No wonder that Angela McRobbie asserts that being a socially intelligible female in today's society "makes one ill."[79] Anorexia, bulimia, and pervasive body anxiety are the pathological underside of neoliberal femininity. As Douglas sums up the matter, "Better to have a little bit of an eating disorder, or a really weird relationship to food, and a hatred of your own body, than defy the whole thinness-beauty regime and be thought of as unattractive (bad), unfeminine (really bad), or a feminist (like totally odious)."[80]

Against this backdrop, Douglas hypothesizes that many postfeminism women miss feminism without realizing it. She proposes that "the 'body by Victoria' ideal" that permeates our culture generates a great deal of semi-acknowledged rage among young women but that, in the absence of feminism, they have no way to verbalize this rage, with the consequence that instead of directing it at heteropatriarchy, they tend to direct it at other women: "Girls have learned to be 'enforcers of their own oppression,' calling each other sluts and whores, imposing even more ridiculous rules on themselves than the beauty-industrial complex does, and mocking girls whose clothes, hair, figures, or social status just aren't right."[81]

This culture of neoliberal femininity easily gives rise to an internalized version of the male gaze: an attitude of constant self-assessment that I've come to think of as "the surveillance gaze." Such a surveillance gaze is relentlessly self-critical, engaged in a continuous comparison between one's appearance and that of other women, and anxiously worried about one's desirability to men. There are obviously young women who have uttered a vehement *no* to this gaze, who are either explicitly rejecting the accouterments of normative femininity or not really thinking about the matter a whole lot. But by many accounts, "looking hot" is a priority for many young women (more on this shortly).

Undoubtedly, women in today's society often adopt a third-person perspective on their own bodies, spending a great deal of time imagining how they appear to others. In 1972, John Berger said, "Men look at women. Women watch themselves being looked at. This determines not only the relations of men to women, but the relations of women to themselves."[82] Not much has changed since then, except that women's tendency to translate the male gaze to a self-scrutinizing, self-policing surveillance gaze has arguably escalated, generating the kind of self-directed sadism that may be even more eroding of self-esteem than the male gaze Mulvey analyzed. And, ironically, this is happening while women are being told that they're finally fully liberated, that they've never had it so good.

To the extent that the female self, in today's consumer culture, is defined in bodily terms, agency becomes recast as a matter of bodily control. Michelle Lazar goes as far as to propose that female liberation has become equated with liberation from physical flaws, noting that advertisements for beauty products often explicitly use "feminist-speak" to present the attainment of bodily perfection as a feminist right (so that instead of fighting, say, for equal pay, you're fighting for your "right" to the perfect body).[83] Likewise, makeover shows market the right to be beautiful at the same time as they explicitly accept the male gaze as a valid measure of female self-worth.

Consider the popular British makeover show *Ten Years Younger* (2004–). Estella Tincknell explains that this show subjects the woman seeking to improve her appearance to a humiliating pre-makeover assessment by (supposedly random) men on the street who invariably guess her to be much older than she actually is:

> This emphasis on the importance of others' evaluations of her, on being judged literally at face value, and on the centrality of to-be-looked-at-ness is, of course, hardly surprising in a makeover show. But the force with which it is directed at these women is chilling. How dare they neglect themselves! No wonder no man wants to marry them! Don't they know that they must keep young and beautiful if they want to be loved?[84]

After each makeover has been accomplished, the "remade" woman is taken back in public, this time with the intent to elicit confirmation from passers-by that her transformation has been successful or, as Tincknell puts it, "to secure the mumbled assurances of what are usually singularly unappealing examples of British masculinity that she is now fuckable."[85] The makeover is here offered as a solution of sorts to "the pathology of femininity—its lack, in an emotional as well as a physical sense."[86]

We've taken a circuitous route back to Lacan. One could argue that now that the body has become the cornerstone of female subjectivity, the quest for wholeness that Lacan theorized and that, according to Silverman, underpins the functioning of cinematic suture, has been reconfigured as a quest for bodily perfection. In this context, consumerism seems to offer the necessary solutions. Through their participation in consumer culture—through developing consumer savvy, purchasing the right products, exchanging tips about what to buy, and so on—women gain the illusion of agency over their being. Finding the right props for femininity in the commercial realm brings a temporary sense of satisfaction, healing lack, suturing fragmentation, completing what seems incomplete. Unfortunately, as neoliberal femininity's ugly sibling of eating disorders reveals, this alleviation of anxiety is always precarious, always threatened by the next chocolate chip cookie.

To sum up the findings of twenty-first-century feminist media scholarship: feminism has been largely supplanted by postfeminism which both commercializes female emancipation and renders it compatible with heteropatriarchy. As Douglas quips, postfeminism sells us the line that "through women's calculated deployment of their faces, bodies, attire, and sexuality they gain and enjoy true power—power that is fun, that men will not resent, and indeed will embrace."[87] True power, in the postfeminist universe, is a matter of getting men to lust after you and other women to envy you.

Sexual self-objectification

Many women are fully aware of the degree to which contemporary body ideals are unrealistic and punishing, yet they are unable to shed the power of these ideals. Frankfurt School scholars Max Horkheimer and Theodor Adorno argued already in 1944 that the ultimate triumph of the advertising industry is when consumers see through the marketing ruse but buy the product anyway.[88] This is one of the predicaments of contemporary womanhood: many women do see through the ruses of media culture but buy its ideals anyway. Moreover, today's women are much less bothered by the male gaze than one might expect in the aftermath of the kinds of feminist critiques I've examined. Precisely because neoliberal femininity promotes self-objectification (women's various attempts to enhance their sex appeal) as empowering, being able to elicit the male gaze has become associated with pleasure and self-confidence.

This approach isn't entirely without logic, for it's true that being able to captivate another person's attention is a form of power. As Elaine Scarry argues, the person whose gaze is arrested by a beautiful object—whether animate or inanimate—in many ways surrenders to that object, allowing himself to be disoriented by his encounter with it.[89] It's not a coincidence that contemporary movies and television shows exploit this power reversal by foregrounding the ways in which women can use their to-be-looked-at-ness to manipulate men. This is why the guy who rides his bicycle into a tree when he sees a stunning woman on the sidewalk is a stock figure of romantic comedies.

I've illustrated that one of the main messages of postfeminist culture is that hypersexualized women may seem objectified but that they are actually on top because in choosing to objectify themselves, they manage reduce men to ogling, stuttering nitwits. But there is another reason for self-objectification that even I can't argue with: it can be a way of rejecting older tropes of female sexual passivity.

I've written extensively about the exasperating stereotypes that our society advances about the lack of female sexual desire in comparison to male desire. If popular scientists and self-help authors are to be believed, women don't have a sexual bone in their bodies; if anything, they find sex vaguely distasteful, something they consent to merely to please men.⁹⁰ The idea that men always want it whereas women rarely do is the foundation of the gender stereotyping enterprise I criticized above. In such a cultural milieu, it's hardly surprising that female self-objectification can seem like a feminist practice. Indeed, as we'll see in the next chapter, *Pretty Woman* was so successful, in part, precisely because it countered the image of the sexually demure woman: whatever else Vivian Ward is, she's not a prude.

In 1990, many female viewers appreciated seeing a sexually assertive woman on the big screen. I still think that *Pretty Woman* was bold in this regard. It's just that now that postfeminism has become the cultural norm, we've seen more than enough female flesh in popular media: we're no longer in the realm of cultural innovation but seem to have looped back into a fairly worn out (predictable) incarnation of heteropatriarchy. This is why Ariel Levy's polemic regarding the hypersexualization of American women in *Female Chauvinist Pigs* (2006) hits a nerve, at least among those of us who know how hard feminists have worked to break the cycle of objectification that has plagued Western women since time immemorial.

Levy analyzes the emergence of raunch culture: a sexually explicit culture where women strive to look like hookers, emulate the sexuality of porn stars, take pole dancing lessons, and compete to appear in *Girls Gone Wild* videos. This culture, Levy proposes, unapologetically advocates "the survival of the skankiest."[91] The problem with it is not that women are being sexual but rather that the terms of their sexuality are, once again, set by a heteropatriarchal society governed by a heteropatriarchal sexual imagination. As Levy explains, despite its appearance of liberation, raunch culture is not "opening our minds to the possibilities and mysteries of sexuality" but merely "endlessly reiterating one particular—and particularly commercial—shorthand for sexiness."[92]

Sexual experimentation—let alone passion—is not the point of raunch culture; rather, looking sexy is. As a matter of fact, there is often an explicit disconnect between looking sexy and sex itself, as when Paris Hilton discloses in a *Rolling Stone* interview that her boyfriends routinely tell her that she's not sexual: "Sexy, but not sexual."[93] Indeed, in a sex tape that was leaked to the internet, Hilton is so bored during intercourse that she takes a cell phone call. As Levy glosses the incident, Hilton "is the perfect sexual celebrity for this moment, because our interest is in the appearance of sexiness, not the existence of sexual pleasure."[94] Within this culture, sexual pleasure—which both second-wave and third-wave feminists thought was an important aspect of female empowerment—is entirely secondary to looking hot.

Levy speculates that women who consent to raunch culture often do so because they want to be seen as one of the guys, to enjoy "the frat party of pop culture."[95] That is, some women aspire to be what Levy calls a "loophole woman,"[96] a woman who is able to find the loophole through which to gain a foothold in a male-dominated world (and thus reap the benefits of this world). The loophole woman "gets" men, gets their sexual obsessions, and doesn't give them a hard time about their sexist attitudes, thereby making them comfortable. Levy observes that women have throughout the ages tried to find various ways to make men comfortable, and that participating in raunch culture is yet another way of doing so, of demonstrating that they're not sexually uptight. Raunch culture, Levy observes, "provides a special opportunity for a woman who wants to prove her mettle," who wants to mark herself as tougher, looser, and funnier than other women.[97]

This is a form of female "empowerment" that is emphatically *not* threatening to men—as demands for social, political, and economic equality can be—and could even be seen to be a fairly desperate attempt to appease male anxieties about the victories of feminism: men now have to put up with female equality in the work force but at least they still get to look at boobs. Indeed, women not only explicitly invite them to look at their boobs but seem willing to join them at the strip joint to admire the boobs of other women. All of this is of course done with a great deal of irony, as a joke, so what could be wrong with it? It signals that a woman is confident, not embarrassed about her sexuality. Only prissy, old-fashioned feminists could condemn it—right?

Levy remarks that because there has been so much misguided maligning of second-wave feminism in our culture—because it has so consistently been misrepresented as antisex, antipleasure, and forbidding—the problem is that, in today's society, women seem to have two equally unpalatable alternatives: either they must buy into a hypersexualized culture that tells them that being fuckable is their most important asset or they must risk being read as being uncomfortable about their sexuality. "Nobody wants to be the frump at the back of the room anymore, a ghost of women past," Levy writes, "It's just not cool."[98] And because there is no space for a feminist critique of dominant forms of heterosexuality, these forms become the only option. Given that the only alternative seems to be a prim sex-negativity, what's a girl to do?

And what's a girl to do in our hyperpornified culture—a culture that seems to kill men's desire with one click of the mouse—but to compete with porn stars? Though cultural hype about men always wanting it is ongoing, anecdotal evidence tells me that some women these days feel that men actually *don't* want it, that their constant porn consumption is so numbing that sex with real women becomes a chore. I've had young men tell me point-blank—because I'm curious enough to ask—that sex with real women is never as good as sex on the internet, that it takes too much effort (you have to try to actually please the woman), and that it's invariably less interesting because there is a limit to what you can do. Plus you have to worry about your performance. In porn, women moan appreciatively if you just touch their hand; in real life, getting them to moan takes some effort. So why bother? Why not just go online and get it over with in a matter of minutes (a neoliberal solution, if there ever was one: maximum reward for minimum exertion)?

Some young women today are up against a peculiar (and arguably a wholly new) problem: they're faced with sexually reluctant men. They're also up against a postfeminist mentality that leaves them little room to protest the omnipresence of heteroporn in our culture. Ironically enough, third-wave feminists, including queer theorists, have contributed to this mentality by suggesting that sexuality in all of its manifestations is subversive and that sexual fantasies shouldn't ever be policed.[99] Although I've always been sympathetic to this point of view, I've recently also come to see that it underestimates the degree to which the multibillion-dollar porn industry that's shaping the sexual imagination of today's straight men is a form of biopolitical control; it overlooks the extent to which mainstream porn is a commercial practice rather than an instrument of sexual liberation.

I'm not saying that porn should be banned. Nor do I think that all porn is patriarchal: I'm aware of feminist, queer, and alternative porn. I'm merely commenting on a sexual landscape that can be confusing—and sometimes even painful—to many women. When men make their female partners feel like it's not okay to complain about their porn consumption—because it, supposedly, "doesn't mean anything"—it feels to me that heteropatriarchy has found yet another way to enact the same tired story: men get to want what they want (in this case, porn) whereas women's preferences are deemed insignificant.

This is why I cannot but agree with Levy that there is something depressing about our postfeminist sexual landscape. As she pointedly asks, "Why is this the 'new feminism' and not what it looks like: the old objectification?"[100] In this way, Levy calls attention to the fact that in postfeminist culture the line between empowerment and disempowerment has gotten terribly blurry. As one of my students put it in a feminist film theory class, it feels a bit like women have given up—discarded feminism—because they've realized that they can't defeat the heteropatriarchal system; the neoliberal pragmatists that they are, they've decided that if they can't beat the system, they might as well join it.

As I suggested earlier, third-wave feminism might have inadvertently contributed to this phenomenon by banking on the power of gender performativity: when agency becomes defined as a matter of reiterating dominant norms, the space for genuine social change shrinks. This is why I have a degree of sympathy for Levy's conviction that the rampant female sexual display of today's culture is a smokescreen for a lack of genuine liberation. As she provocatively adds:

> The proposition that having the most simplistic, plastic stereotypes of female sexuality constantly reiterated throughout our culture somehow proves that we are sexually liberated and personally empowered has been offered to us, and we have accepted it. But if we think about it, we know this just doesn't make any sense. It's time to stop nodding and smiling uncomfortably as we ignore the crazy feeling in our heads.[101]

Are we all equally objectified?

Rejecting the equation of female empowerment with female sexual objectification can be hard to do in the context of a media culture that normalizes this objectification, that in fact—as Jessica Ringrose states in the course of her analysis of makeover shows—teaches it "as a 'science' to be learned."[102] And it can also be hard to do given that a quick glance at our popular culture reveals that men are, these days, objectified almost as much as women. A survey of television shows—particularly ones aimed at young audiences—immediately illustrates the contemporary appeal of the shirtless man. The young men of *The Vampire Diaries* (2009–), for instance, spend much of the series half-naked—hypocritically, even I'm not complaining. And who can forget the immense poster of David Beckham in nothing but tight Armani skivvies gracing Times Square?

In some ways, the playing field has been leveled. It would be easy to argue that we're now all equally objectified, that there isn't much of a difference between a pair of cut-off shorts barely covering a woman's ass on a poster and the Armani briefs that barely covered (in fact more like *outlined*) Beckham's penis. Still, it's not entirely obvious that we're talking about comparable instances. In her reading of the Beckham ad, Rosalind Gill notes that there might have been a fair amount of "shock and awe and phallus worship" in the mix.[103]

Beckham wasn't displayed merely in order to incite female (and gay male) desire but also in order to be admired for his impeccable performance, proven on the soccer field as well as (the ad left us no doubt about this) in the bedroom. Victoria Beckham in fact announced in an interview that she was "proud to see his penis 25 feet tall. It's enormous. Massive."[104] This implies that male sexual display may still have a different valence from female sexual display: if the latter always risks sliding into denigration, the former could easily slide into cock worship.

There is no denying that contemporary advertising—and media culture, broadly understood—routinely breaks the old dichotomy of man as bearer of the look and woman as its object. Young, fit, and beautiful male bodies are offered for our consumption. Yet image makers also use various strategies to mitigate the threat this poses for masculine prowess. As Gill explains, media images of men often emphasize their power along with their desirability: muscled, unsmiling men stare boldly at the viewer, asserting dominance. If women strike poses that connote submission—such as lying down, looking down, or smiling invitingly—men tend to stand up and look directly at the camera. This is one reason the Beckham ad is so interesting: though he meets the viewer's gaze straight on, he's pictured lying down, in an overtly sexualized (and passive) pose.

It's of course also the case that women in media photos are now more likely than they were twenty years ago to confidently return the viewer's gaze. Indeed, media images routinely display women not merely as sexualized but also as assertive, independent, playful, and even aggressive. Yet, as Gill remarks, displays of female empowerment can sometimes work as an alibi for representations that, without them, might be accused of sexism. In general, the claim that men and women are now equally objectified can be used to silence concerns about the representation of women. In the same way as the profusion of kind, gentle, and emotionally available young men in television shows can be used to claim that feminism has run its course—what are you worried about if men are this sweet?— the depiction of women as assertive can be used to justify their continued objectification.

Once again, it would be hard to wish for a return to the earlier status quo. It seems like progress that many men on television these days are nonsexist—"touched by feminism,"[105] as Douglas puts it—and that, in comparison, the sexist ones seem hopelessly undesirable. And it seems like progress that women in magazine ads are allowed to stare back at the viewer with a degree of assertiveness. It would certainly be reasonable to propose that these developments both reflect a positive change in our culture and contribute to it.

Moreover, as Mark Simpson maintains, the objectification of men may represent a fracturing of heteropatriarchy in the sense that men being displayed for an "undifferentiated" gaze represents a direct challenge to both male dominance and heteronormativity: "Traditional male heterosexuality, which insists that it's always active, sadistic and desiring is now inundated by images of men's bodies as passive, masochistic and desired. Narcissism, the desire to be desired, once regarded as a feminine quality par excellence, is, it seems, in popular culture at least, now more often associated with men than women."[106]

Gill agrees, suggesting that although phenomena like the Beckham ad can be seen as bolstering patriarchy, on some level they also erode its confidence. To illustrate her point, Gill quotes male commentators on the ad who admit that it has the potential to make "an entire gender feel inadequate" and that, consequently, "being reduced to a quivering jelly of insecurity is no longer just for women."[107] All of this can be interpreted to mean that we now live in a more egalitarian world. Yet the general tenor of this world—good or bad?—defies straightforward assessment.

Why *Pretty Woman*?

If it appears that we're very far from the world of *Pretty Woman*—the analysis of which will take up the next chapter—let us recall that the movie arguably started it all by introducing the "hooker look." Bloomingdale's subsequently made this look available to well-scrubbed middle-class girls by marketing a replica of the knee-high boots that Julia Roberts wears for the first half of the movie (these came to be known as "the Pretty Woman boots"). Let us also recall that *Pretty Woman* is a movie where Richard Gere's body is almost as strongly objectified as that of Roberts. It helped that Gere came to *Pretty Woman* from movies such as *American Gigolo* (1980) and *Internal Affairs* (1990), which had generously displayed his body for an avid straight female audience, which had deliberately accentuated his "to-be-looked-at-ness," with the result that the visual imprint of his previous work haunts the buttoned-up Edward he plays in *Pretty Woman*, constantly threatening to blow the lid on his repressed upper-crust properness.

Furthermore, the pose Edward strikes in the movie's first sex scene—when he's about to receive a blowjob from Roberts's Vivian—is remarkable similar to that of Beckham in the Armani ad, with Edward reclining in a chair, his upper body bare and his tight underwear hinting at male potency about to leap to life. This scene, like the Beckham ad, could in fact be characterized as containing a strong subtext of cock worship, for it shows Vivian approaching Edward on her knees, like a sexual supplicant begging for a chance to apply her magic touch to his knightly shaft. Indeed, one of *Pretty Woman*'s underlying messages to women could be said to be that knowing how to give a hooker-grade blowjob will get you a marriage proposal from a billionaire (who also happens to be a gentleman).

However, if this were the sum total of the movie's message, I wouldn't have chosen it as the case study for the next chapter, the purpose of which is to illustrate how feminist film theory can be applied to Hollywood romantic comedies. I selected *Pretty Woman* from among many possibilities because its engagement with feminism is surprisingly nuanced. On the one hand, it showcases many of the problematic themes I've discussed in this chapter, such as the male gaze, the masquerade of femininity, neoliberal happiness scripts, the valorization of marriage, ostentatious consumerism, and female self-objectification. On the other, released in 1990—in the immediate aftermath of second-wave feminism—it contains many elements of embedded feminism. For instance, although Vivian revels in self-objectification, explicitly inviting the male gaze, she's also spirited, autonomous, sexually assertive, and—as I already noted in the Introduction—openly defiant of dominant social conventions.

For these reasons, *Pretty Woman* can't easily be categorized as either antifeminist or feminist but rather illustrates the complex negotiation of retrograde and progressive themes that, more broadly, characterizes the postfeminist cultural terrain. My sense is that it's this aspect of the movie—perhaps even more than its fairytale romance—that accounts for its immense popularity among female viewers. In the course of writing this book, I talked with a number of women who enthusiastically claimed that they could cite much of its dialogue from memory. "Well, color me happy. There's a sofa in here for two" seemed to be a favorite line, in close competition with "Fifty bucks, grandpa. For seventy-five, the wife can watch." In the pages that follow, I'll try to understand why *Pretty Woman* made such an impact, why these lines have stuck in the minds of women across the years.

CHAPTER TWO

Feminist Film Theory and *Pretty Woman*

At first glance, the plot of *Pretty Woman* doesn't promise much feminist satisfaction. Small-town girl Vivian Ward (Julia Roberts) moves from Georgia to Los Angeles, falls on hard times, and ends up prostituting herself on Hollywood Boulevard. One night—but well before Vivian's youthful innocence has been washed into the gutter—a jaded business mogul from New York, Edward Lewis (Richard Gere), asks her for directions to Beverly Hills. Lest there's any doubt that Edward is a desirable customer, the audience has just learned that Vivian is desperately short of cash because her roommate Kit (Laura San Giacomo) has spent their rent on party drugs. So Vivian hops in the flashy Lotus Esprit Edward has borrowed from his lawyer, Phil (Jason Alexander), in the hope of earning back the money.

It turns out that Edward, who is used to a world of limos, doesn't know how to handle a stick shift, so Vivian drives him to his hotel, the opulent Regent Beverly Wilshire. Though Edward initially has no interest in hiring a prostitute, one thing leads to another—to a blowjob, more specifically—and Vivian ends up spending the night. The next morning, Edward asks her to spend the week as his companion to various business-related events, specifying that he wants a professional because he doesn't want any "romantic hassles." For this service, Vivian is paid the (to her) whopping sum of three thousand dollars (the movie's original title was *Three Thousand Dollars*).

In order to pull off her role as Edward's companion, Vivian—who at the beginning of the movie wears a revealing, overtly sexy outfit that instantly codes her as a hooker—needs to undergo a drastic makeover. First up is Edward's business dinner at the elegant Voltaire with Mr. Morse (Ralph Bellamy), the elderly and upright businessman Edward is courting in the hope of taking over his company and selling it off piece by piece for profit. In preparation for the dinner, Edward sends Vivian to Rodeo Drive to buy a suitable outfit, but Vivian—still dressed like a hooker—finds that the snobbish sales personnel in the snobbish boutiques that line the street deem her to be an unsuitable customer and refuse to serve her.

Fortunately, the kind manager of the Regent—the inimitable Hector Elizondo as Mr. Thompson—rescues Vivian from further humiliation by providing her with the necessary black cocktail dress and by teaching her the tricks of fine dining (e.g., how to recognize a salad fork). The dinner presents some obstacles, for Vivian doesn't recognize the fancy dishes Edward orders for her, can't figure out the silverware (she only knows the salad fork), and sends an escargot flying into the anticipatory hand of a waiter standing on alert for embarrassing lapses such as this. But Mr. Morse is charmed by Vivian's lack of high-society manners, announcing that he also has trouble telling one fork from another. An immediate affinity is therefore established between Mr. Morse—the businessman with a heart of gold—and Vivian, the hooker with a heart of gold.

The next morning, Edward finds out about Vivian's mortification on Rodeo Drive and, infuriated, accompanies her to an expensive store. Armed with a MasterCard and a brass Manhattan attitude, Edward announces to the store manager than his sales crew has some "major sucking up" to do, specifying that it's Vivian, and not himself, that is to be the object of this sucking up. When the store manager deferentially asks how much money he plans to spend, Edward specifies that it's going to be an "offensive" amount.

What follows is a makeover scene that miraculously—as is the way of fairytales—transforms Vivian from a hooker to a "lady." It turns out that clothes really do make a woman, for when Vivian walks out of the boutique, wearing a stylish sundress and carrying shopping bags filled with other character-defining garments, passers-by, including well-dressed men, look at her with deep admiration rather than with the disapproval that had met her hooker incarnation the previous day. Vivian confidently walks into one of the stores that had refused to serve her during her earlier shopping expedition and asks the sales women if they remember her. When they, with a degree of confusion, indicate that they don't, she raises her shopping bags, uttering a triumphant "Big mistake. Big. Huge!"

Next, we accompany Vivian to various high-class functions, the culmination of which is a night at the San Francisco Opera, where Edward—how else?—flies her in his private jet. But before Edward and Vivian board the jet, viewers are given the pleasure of seeing Edward escort Vivian through the lobby of the Regent, where all eyes fixate on the utterly altered Vivian. She's wearing a fabulous red gown and a ruby necklace worth a quarter of a million dollars that Edward has borrowed for the evening. As Vivian glides from one end of the lobby to the other, she convinces everyone, including Edward, that she is a worthy companion for him.

Her physical transformation complete, Vivian is now free to express her "true" self: it turns out that she was never really a hooker at heart but rather a thoroughly upright girl who is able to appreciate the finer pleasures of life. This becomes apparent at the opera, for Vivian—despite having never seen an opera before—instantly falls in love with it (the irony of her watching Verdi's *La Traviata*, an opera about the tragic fate of a prostitute, is lost on her because she doesn't know Italian). In this manner, Vivian is revealed to be Edward's soul mate, for Edward—as is fitting for a New York socialite—is an opera buff: it's Vivian's emotional reaction to opera (she both delights in it and, appropriately, cries at the sad parts) that allows him to develop a romantic interest in her.

As we watch the romance between them develop, Edward comes to respect Vivian as his equal and she, as has always been the mysterious way of women, humanizes him, transforming him from a bloodthirsty destroyer of companies to a man who wants to "build something." At the end, Edward joins forces with Mr. Morse to rescue his company and even learns to value Vivian's low-class (but oh-so-human) amusements, such as walking barefoot on grass. Somewhere along the line, he reminds Vivian that prostitution is not her only option—that she could "be so much more"—with the result that she decides to go back to school.

Edward and Vivian part ways after their "contract" comes to an end. But when checking out of the Regent on this way back to New York, Edward is brought to his senses by Mr. Thompson, who, admiring the necklace that Vivian had worn to the opera, remarks that it must be painful for Edward to let go of "something so beautiful." Ostensibly, they're talking about the necklace—which Edward has asked Mr. Thompson to return to the store—but they both know that they're talking about Vivian (who is therefore explicitly equated with the expensive necklace).

Edward realizes that he's in love with Vivian and, instead of heading to the airport, asks his limo driver to take him to her apartment. He arrives there riding his white limo like a knight on a white steed and courageously jabbing the air with his dragon-slaying sword, a.k.a. his umbrella. As his limo driver watches with obvious amusement, he starts to climb up the fire escape to Vivian's apartment. Vivian knows that he suffers from a fear of heights so, out of mercy, she descends to meet him half way. Handing her a bouquet of red roses, and aware of his role as a fairytale prince rescuing a princess from her tower, he asks what happens after she has been rescued. "She rescues him right back," Vivian responds.

"She rescues him right back" is a striking ending for a traditional fairytale. Indeed, as the enthusiastic reception of the gutsy heroine of Disney's *Frozen* (2014)—who also "rescues" her man as much as she is rescued by him—revealed, the concept has lost none of its power to enchant female audiences even a quarter of a century later. Interestingly, what *has* changed is the reaction of movie critics to this plot twist: while many critics praised *Frozen* for its "updated" gender politics, *Pretty Woman* was fairly unanimously slammed for its mutual rescue fantasy by both mainstream and academic critics.

One can certainly see why. *Pretty Woman*, after all, offers a modern rendition of the Cinderella story with a hefty serving of ingredients borrowed from *My Fair Lady* (1964), where Henry Higgins fashions a lady out of the poor flower girl Eliza Doolittle. It also contains clear echoes of Ovid's *Metamorphoses* (8 AD), where Pygmalion carves an ivory statue of a woman who warms to his touch and becomes his loving bride Galatea. That all of these stories center on the fashioning of a perfect woman—a woman who meets the requirements of femininity as heteropatriarchy has defined it—was not lost on critics, who deemed *Pretty Woman*'s basic message to be the same as that of *Vertigo*, namely that it takes a man to make the perfect woman (the important difference being that Garry Marshall is no Hitchcock). Nor was the movie's glamorization of prostitution and celebration of Reagan-era conspicuous consumption embraced by its critics.

As will become clear in the course of my analysis, I agree with some of the criticisms leveled against the movie in the years immediately after its release. Yet it also feels that the movie's early critics were so focused on its obviously retrograde aspects that they missed (or misjudged) the elements of its plot that spoke to female audiences hungry for role models of female independence. Though *Pretty Woman* is by no means a feminist movie, it spices up its romance with themes that foreground female autonomy and competence. As I argued in the previous chapter, this is one of the defining qualities of modern romantic comedies (for which *Pretty Woman* in many ways offered the prototype). Given that—as I've emphasized—there may be something potentially misogynistic about the blanket condemnation of such movies, it seems important to attempt to understand why so many women find them appealing. As a result, in the analysis that follows, I'll try to foreground the quasi-feminist and frankly feminist elements of *Pretty Woman* without losing track of the features that critics have justifiably found problematic.

The attack of early critics

When *Pretty Woman* was released, mainstream movie critics descended upon it like a flock of vultures, ready to tear it apart limb by limb. Dennis Delgrough of the *LA Weekly* accused director Garry Marshall of projecting "his *My Fair Lady* concept as a derisive male fantasy: whore regenerated as ideal woman, one who shops." David Sterritt of the *Christian Science Monitor* blamed the movie for endorsing patriarchy: "The message is plain: Men, especially rich men, have all the power." Desson Howe of the *Washington Post* condemned "the movie's capitalistically lurid aspects." Henry Sheehan of the *Reader* concurred, ridiculing to the movie's "infantile pleasure in unfettered materialism." And Janet Maslin of the *New York Times* claimed that "everything in the movie has a price tag."

Owen Gleiberman of *Entertainment Weekly* concluded that the movie presents "the kinds of characters who exist nowhere but in the minds of callowly manipulative Hollywood screenwriters." Jonathan Rosenbaum of *Chicagoreader.com* remarked that the movie "proves that the Disney people can sell just about anything—including a misogynistic celebration of big business and prostitution." Peter Travers of *Rolling Stone* predicted that you might like the movie, "but you'll hate yourself in the morning." Finally, Sheila Benson of the *Los Angeles Times* concluded that "nothing works, except perhaps the sight of Julia Roberts' lean, well-tempered midsection and her roughly eight yards of legs that, in this frail comedy, are worked until they're almost a story point of their own." Benson's judgment is particularly amusing, given that Roberts's body double—Shelley Michelle—is reported as stating that the studio wanted to use a double because Roberts's legs were not attractive enough: "Julia has these straight legs and they wanted somebody shapely."[1]

Roger Ebert dared to disagree with the general assessment, asserting that *Pretty Woman* "glows with romance," and characterizing its leading lady as "a woman who is as smart as she is attractive, which makes her very smart." Ebert also correctly predicted that the movie would make Roberts a star, specifying that Roberts "gives her character an irrepressibly bouncy sense of humor and then lets her spend the movie trying to repress it. Actresses who can do that and look great can have whatever they want in Hollywood."[2]

Ebert wasn't alone in recognizing Roberts's superstar potential, for even those who panned the movie tended to give credit to her performance. Maslin admitted that Roberts is "so enchantingly beautiful, so funny, so natural and such an absolute delight that it is hard to hold anything against the movie." Howe likewise praised Roberts's "ticklishly appealing" performance, specifying that her comic timing "is the most distinguishing aspect of the movie." Even Travers begrudgingly conceded that "the Roberts smile—full-lipped, a mile wide and gleaming—is the closest the movies have yet come to capturing sunshine," forecasting that in years to come, Hollywood historians would be able to "pinpoint the precise moment when Julia Roberts became a star": "about fifteen minutes into this silly-shallow comedy."

While the performances of Hector Elizondo and Laura San Giacomo were generally praised, and while some critics reluctantly acknowledged that Gere's performance was dapper and amusing, director Garry Marshall was fairly consistently condemned for replacing the social criticism of J. F. Lawton's original script—which was designed to draw a stark parallel between prostitution and corporate raiding—with an unrealistic fairytale romance. This aspect of the movie's history—that it was initially written to be a social commentary rather than a "mere" romantic comedy—may explain why it includes relatively rough scenes that aren't part of the usual romcom repertoire: a murder investigation, drug dealing, poverty, homelessness, prostitution, an (off-screen) blowjob, and even Roberts's exposed nipple. These are themes that more recent romantic comedies avoid.

For instance, though many twenty-first-century romcoms play with the rags-to-riches Cinderella motif, their depictions of poverty tend to be more Disnified than the poverty of *Pretty Woman*. Likewise, their sexuality tends to be PG rather than R-rated: that *Pretty Woman* starts the romance between Edward and Vivian with a blowjob reveals the hesitation of the production team about what kind of a movie it was going to be, for this is, by all accounts, an uncharacteristic starting point for the kind of happily ever after that romcoms, generally speaking, are after. That many early critics of the movie would have preferred it to remain a social critique is interesting in itself, perhaps having to do with the low status of romcoms that I've called attention to.

Early scholarly assessments of *Pretty Woman* mirror its negative reception among mainstream critics. Scholars had three principal reasons for condemning it: (1) its recycling of retrograde, antifeminist messages about gender; (2) its ethos of capitalist greed and over-the-top consumption; and (3) its unrealistic portrayal of prostitution as alluring rather than misery inducing. For example, Karol Kelley, comparing *Pretty Woman* to earlier versions of the Cinderella story, asserts that the movie "does not illustrate any major changes in gender expectations and is unaffected by any form of feminist ideology."[3] Along related lines, D. Soyini Madison maintains that *Pretty Woman* resolves social anxieties concerning social class and women's autonomy "by ultimately upholding traditional, hegemonic conceptions and practices regarding marriage, chivalry, and consumer capitalism."[4] Claude Smith in turn remarks that "throughout the film, Viv is weak, dependent, and essentially helpless to fend for herself" whereas the movie's men, in contrast, "are superior in social position, wealth, power, autonomy, and general competence."[5]

The points of Kelley and Madison are reasonable but Smith's assessment of Vivian's character is harder to defend: as I'll show below, Vivian is far from being weak, dependent, and helpless. However, what is most interesting about Smith's reading is the moralistic tone that rapidly takes over his analysis. This tone is notable—if still somewhat muted—in his condemnation of Vivian's "peasant manners": "Although she unbelievably speaks standard English instead of cracker dialect, she is, nevertheless, ignorant poor white trash."[6] Moreover, apparently forgetting that he's talking about a movie that explicitly markets itself as a comedy, Smith is astonished that Edward doesn't find Vivian flinging a snail across the Voltaire in the least bit "repugnant or embarrassing."[7] But it's in relation to the movie's depiction of female sexuality that Smith's moralistic tone reaches a genuinely disapproving pitch. Approvingly quoting another critic's assessment of Vivian as an Audrey Hepburn who gives good head, Smith deems Vivian "seedy merchandise" and wonders why "Vivian's total sexual abandon" doesn't diminish Edward's estimate of her.[8]

Should it?

Smith proceeds to accuse *Pretty Woman* of implying that whoring is "good, clean, profitable fun," explaining that its portrayal of prostitution "belies the truth about prostitutes: many are runaways who start selling themselves at fourteen and who suffer sexual abuse and a dependency on drugs."[9] Complaining that the movie suggests that "only expensive clothing separates whores from married and/or professional women," Smith labels its plot as "ludicrous in light of the research showing that prostitutes focus so much on commercial relations that they have difficulty in forming close relations."[10] Finally, regarding the union of Edward and Vivian at the end of the movie, Smith protests that "we do not examine the social ostracism they would encounter nor the potential she has for child-bearing, nor STDs, nor social class differences, nor any aspect of the real world."[11]

Smith's disparaging commentary on "whoring," STDs, and Vivian's child-bearing potential—not to mention his demand for a "realistic" portrayal of prostitution—seems rather bizarre in the context of a Hollywood romcom. But he's not alone in taking the moral high road. Harvey Roy Greenberg goes as far as to wonder whether *Pretty Woman*'s popularity among "legions of female viewers"—women's enigmatic willingness to ignore its "repellant sexist themes"—could be due to false consciousness.[12] "Perhaps they are unaware of the film's Neanderthal intentions," Greenberg suggests, for otherwise he finds it difficult to explain why "a surprising number of women with feminist backgrounds or sensibility, *knowing that they should know better*, still have greatly—if guiltily— enjoyed *Pretty Woman*."[13]

Aware that accusing "legions" of women, let alone feminists, of false consciousness might come too close to the very misogyny he seeks to condemn, Greenberg hypothesizes that *Pretty Woman*'s success may be explained by the "stringency" of contemporary women's lot: in Greenberg's view, the grim realities of gender inequality, feminine poverty, the hardships of single-mother families, and the quotidian drudgeries of marriage provide a "spur for outworn fantasies of rescue by an omnipotent, wealthy hunk *cum* patriarch to flourish."[14] In this manner, Greenberg explains *Pretty Woman*'s popularity by women's general "exhaustion of spirit," by "disillusion given way to eroticized illusion of a better life through the dubious blandishments of pennydreadful romance."[15]

Greenberg moreover seems to believe that female viewers are moronic enough to be completely duped by the devious work of the "cinematic apparatus" that seeks to obscure the movie's "dominant bourgeois ideology."[16] Elizabeth Scala wryly observes in response that it's hard to see how women could possibly be blinded in this way, given that "'dominant bourgeois ideology' is hardly effaced in this film, which appears so self-consciously concerned with shopping and spending in almost every scene."[17] Such considerations, however, do not deter Greenberg from claiming that *Pretty Woman* "veils its exploitative agenda with fashionably feminist leftover blather."[18]

According to Greenberg, the only thing worse about *Pretty Woman* than its celebration of conspicuous consumption is its (related) celebration of patriarchy: "In the daisy chain of possession energized by Edward's phallic mastercard, Vivian herself has become an extension of this consummate prick's prick, synecdoche of his potency, the more desirable for miming his obscenely extravagant expenditures."[19] Derisively noting that Vivian's "harlotry is clearly provisional until some prince climbs her tower," Greenberg asserts that her role in Edward's marriage script is to "be abiding cheerfully at home—an icon of passivity in a one-gal harem—waiting to service the sahib."[20] Portraying Vivian as a "decerebrate dingaling" whose vulgarity "could gag a goat," Greenberg bleakly concludes that "in choosing her prince, and the tainted fairytale he incarnates, Vivian has simply exchanged one form of whoring for another."[21]

Should women know better?

Though there are elements of Greenberg's interpretation that are insightful—such as his recognition that Vivian's status as a prostitute is clearly provisional from the get-go—in the analysis that follows, I try to offer a more balanced reading of the film, not the least because I believe that female viewers usually do know better. In other words, Greenberg's assessment, like that of Smith, is problematic in implying that women's relationship to romcoms is more naïve than, say, men's relationship to action thrillers, that unlike male viewers, who can tell fantasy from reality, who know that they'll never be Bruce Wayne of the Batman series, women who watch *Pretty Woman* deep down expect to be rescued from the boredom of their lives by a mild-mannered billionaire who looks like Richard Gere.

Are Tom Cruise's *Mission: Impossible* movies somehow more "lifelike" than *Pretty Woman*? Is Daniel Craig's James Bond more "truthful" than Julia Roberts's Vivian? In a Hollywood milieu where no one is accusing action films, thrillers, sci-fi movies, hangover romps, or other "masculine" genres of unrealistic depiction, asking a Garry Marshall romcom to present life "as it really is" smacks of a misogynistic double standard.

It's of course true that none of us can fully escape the biopolitical conditioning that Hollywood carries out: there is no question that *Pretty Woman*, like other romcoms, sells us the dominant happiness scripts of our society, promoting a very specific vision of the good life, a vision that revolves around romance, marriage, and buying things. Madison is right to posit that *Pretty Woman* advances a myth that American women have historically found hard to resist: "A beautiful girl, stigmatized in some way, is rescued and thereby actualized by a handsome, rich, adoring man."[22] And she may even be right to assert that, as a major producer of cultural symbols, Disney films have "the potential to reflect, enhance, and subvert our understandings of our real lifeworlds as well as our fantasies."[23]

But I wouldn't go as far as to argue, as Madison does, that *Pretty Woman* constricts "the aspirations, life goals, and imaginations of all women."[24] Even though I've emphasized that there is a limit to the degree to which we can resist normative happiness scripts—that even a stance of ironic distance doesn't necessarily keep these scripts from infiltrating our psychic lives—I wouldn't want to overstate the matter, for I don't believe that female spectators walk out of the movie theater (or turn off their Blu-ray players) entirely hoodwinked. If anything, the preachy tone of critics such as Smith and Greenberg—a tone that depicts female viewers as passive idiots undergoing a thorough patriarchal brainwashing—is arguably more offensive than the content of *Pretty Woman*. I would hypothesize that many women like romcoms not because they believe that Richard Gere will one day "climb their tower" but because the heroines of these movies are usually *not* "decerebrate dingalings."

I've already noted that *Pretty Woman* includes enough messages about female empowerment to speak to female spectators looking for images of gender equality. As a consequence, a feminist analysis of the movie should perhaps focus less on its alleged misogyny than on *the version of female empowerment* it endorses. In this regard, there is admittedly much to criticize. Released at the threshold of postfeminism, *Pretty Woman* equates female empowerment with sexual display, bodily transformation, and consumer savvy. As we saw in the last chapter, this approach can placate both heteropatriarchy and capitalism by replacing second-wave feminist ideals of radical social change by more individualistic themes of striving and self-improvement. In this manner, it feeds the American habit of translating social problems into personal ones, of offering the promise of upward mobility as a solution to collective inequalities.

That *Pretty Woman* propagates this neoliberal ideology is beyond question, which is perhaps why it garnered the wrath of critics writing in the immediate aftermath of the more politicized discourse of second-wave feminism. Yet it also seems to me that what Greenberg calls the movie's "leftover feminist blather" contains enough elements of embedded feminism to reflect the genuine inroads that second-wave feminism had made in altering the gendered landscape of American society. *Pretty Woman* may sell radical feminist ideals down the river in order to promote a neoliberal version of female empowerment, but it still exhibits too many second-wave feminist ideals to be easily categorizable as antifeminist.

Equally importantly, *Pretty Woman* foreshadowed third-wave feminist ideals, such as the softening of the gender binary, in ways that may have increased its long-term popularity; it foretold some of the social trends that were to pick up steam in the decades after its release. In addition, it set the pattern for later romantic comedies by offering a strong female protagonist who was willing to do "whatever it takes" to achieve her goal. This is obviously a version of neoliberal ideology. But against the historical record of gender inequality that had suppressed women's ambitions, it can't be dismissed as a completely retrograde fantasy. We can criticize it until we're blue in the face, but the truth is that it is, for good reasons, more appealing to many female viewers than the 1950s happiness script of married domesticity. For all these reasons, *Pretty Woman*'s message about gender is by no means straightforward: despite its fairytale aspects, it arguably deconstructs traditional gender roles as much as—and perhaps even more than—it reifies them.

In many romantic comedies from the twenty-first century, such as *Miss Congeniality* (2000), *Legally Blonde* (2001), *The Wedding Planner* (2001), *Maid in Manhattan* (2002), *Two Weeks Notice* (2002), *The Devil Wears Prada* (2006), and *Pitch Perfect* (2012), the leading lady's career success is all-important—perhaps more important than her romantic success. If *Pretty Woman* still intertwined the neoliberal success script with the more traditional marriage script, later romcoms tend to create more distance between the two, emphasizing that the driven heroine can succeed even without a man. Still, *Pretty Woman* went a long way in establishing the female happiness script as being *akin* to the male happiness script: as we'll see below, Vivian and Edward are presented as being cut from the same cloth. In a culture prone to relentless gender stereotyping, this is no trifle.

Nor is the movie's treatment of class divisions, capitalist greed, and conspicuous consumption completely backward. There is no denying that money—and the extravagant spending that a surplus of money facilitates—is perhaps the movie's most consistent theme. Yet the fact that the film was initially written as a critique of the ruthlessness of corporate capitalism isn't entirely erased in its final version. This is why I don't think that its early critics are correct in suggesting that it straightforwardly endorses avarice, what Howe labels as "the utterly depressing, materialistic nature of life on Rodeo Drive (and, by vague extension, America)." Rather, I want to illustrate that it condemns the excesses of consumption at the same time as it seduces the viewer with its splendor. More specifically, it keeps flipping the coin so that it can play both sides of the game, repeatedly ridiculing the very wealth that it simultaneously celebrates (and vice versa).

These contradictions—the contradictions of gender and the contradictions of money—are a good place to start a closer examination of the movie. I begin with the theme of money, including the racial politics of upward politics. I then proceed with the theme of gender, focusing on the potentially feminist aspects of the movie, such as its obvious resistance to dominant gender roles. This part of my analysis offers a much more positive interpretation of *Pretty Woman* than its early critics did. However, toward the end of this chapter I return to themes, such as the masquerade of femininity, the male gaze, and fetishism, that are harder to reconcile with feminism. My hope is that by providing a number of different perspectives, my account will illustrate why romantic comedies are difficult to categorize as either antifeminist or feminist. At the very least, I hope to give the reader a starting point for the study of other romantic comedies.

The haves and the have-nots ("It's all about money")

"No matter what they say, it's all about money" is the opening line of *Pretty Woman*, spoken by a magician at a lavish patio party thrown by Phil. This is appropriate given that, besides romance, money is the movie's main preoccupation. One could even say that money is a bigger preoccupation in the movie than romance. However, it's important that—despite the conspicuous consumption that critics have been so quick to latch onto—the movie's first message about money is that it hasn't made Edward happy.

This is of course a tremendous cliché—so much so that one might justifiably feel tired of listening to rich people whine about the lack of fulfillment in their lives. Nevertheless, it seems to me that before we jump to conclusions about female audiences being duped by outworn fantasies of being rescued by an omnipotent patriarch, we should consider the cinematic appeal of the much more realistic theme of wealthy people who, despite their affluence, remain miserable: it might be that women struggling to make a living are more comforted by the idea that money can't ultimately buy satisfaction than by the wholly untenable dream of being yanked from Hollywood Boulevard—or from a garment factory, fast-food joint, or cleaning company—by a tycoon with a sensitive side.

We learn in *Pretty Woman*'s first few minutes that Edward is a workaholic who can't take the time to enjoy his wealth: his character is introduced in a sequence in which he breaks up with his New York-based girlfriend on the phone, chastises one of his assistants for enjoying Phil's party rather than checking on the status of the Tokyo stock market, and flees the party—where he's supposed to be the guest of honor—in Phil's car. Equally importantly, we learn that although women flock to him—after all, he is not just wealthy but also handsome—he doesn't know how to make relationships work. During their phone conversation, his girlfriend accuses him of taking her for granted, of making her feel like she's "at his beck and call." "I talk to your secretary more than I talk to you," she complains.

When Edward moments later runs into an ex-girlfriend at the party, he asks her, "When you and I were dating, did you talk to my secretary more than you spoke to me?" She gives him a knowing look, responding, "She was one of my bridesmaids." In this manner, Edward is established as a successful man who keeps making a mess of his private life. It's not exactly that he treats his girlfriends badly—his ex clearly likes him—but that he's so focused on making money that he neglects life's other aspects. In this way, the audience is invited to sympathize with him despite his obvious privilege: he may be rich but he still has problems, just like the rest of us.

The film's opening sequence also offers an overt commentary on social inequality by foregrounding the stark distinction between Edward's affluent world of business deals, opulent parties, and expensive tickets to the Met on the one hand, and Vivian's world of prostitution, violence, crime, and going hungry on the other. While Edward is abusing the transmission of Phil's expensive car and getting lost in Hollywood, we're introduced to Vivian, who wakes up in her shabby room in a low-rent hotel. I'll return to the opening shots of her body—crucial for the movie's depiction of femininity—later. At this point, let's merely note the details that signal the squalor in which she lives: her hotel is so cheap that half of its neon-lit sign is extinguished; when she discovers that Kit has taken their rent money, Vivian climbs down the fire escape so as to avoid her landlord; on the way to find Kit, she runs into a detective investigating the murder of a prostitute found dead in a dumpster; and her thigh-high boots are so scruffy that she uses a black magic marker to cover over the bald spots. Her first exchange with Kit—the first words she speaks—expresses her anxiety about the missing rent money. Kit, in turn, is shown to snack on the garnishes—olives, cherries, pickled onions, and wedges of orange—that the bartender at their local hangout uses to mix drinks because she has spent all their money on drugs.

The opening sequence also uses atmospheric backdrops to accentuate the difference between the worlds inhabited by Edward and Vivian: Phil's party exudes wealth; Vivian's part of Hollywood Boulevard is filled with distressed prostitutes, aggressive pimps, drug dealers, and cheap restaurants. When Edward enters this scene, he's clearly out of place. He asks a homeless man rummaging in a garbage can (played by director Garry Marshall) for directions to Beverly Hills. The man responds—pleasantly enough but with obvious sarcasm—"You're here. That's Sylvester Stallone's house right there."

Early critics tended to fault *Pretty Woman* for raising social issues only to trivialize them. Madison's assessment is representative. She accuses the movie of ignoring "the realities of drugs, murdered prostitutes and the exploitation on Hollywood Boulevard": "Any hints of underclass grime or crime are glossed over as the film quickly shifts to the glitter and glamor of the 'haves'."[25] On some level, this critique is clearly valid. Yet it also suffers from the same problem as critiques of the movie, such as Smith's, that approach it with statistics regarding prostitution: it applies to the movie standards that seem as out of place as the demand that action movies depict "realistic" driving scenes rather than the out-of-control chase scenes that are their standard fare.

If anything, looking at *Pretty Woman* a quarter of a century after its release, and comparing it to more recent romcoms—which tend to be discreet about the brutalities of capitalism—I would say that one of its most striking characteristics is not that it obfuscates social inequalities but that it fairly insistently calls attention to them. Its contrast between the haves and the have-nots is obviously essential for Vivian's Cinderella story. But this contrast is drawn much more dramatically than one might expect from a romantic comedy. Indeed, one could argue that social inequality is the premise upon which the movie's entire plot is built, for it creates a clash of worldviews that is then played out in the personal relationship between Edward and Vivian.

This clash of worldviews is produced not only by the opening sequence that I've just described but also by the scene in which Vivian gets her first glimpse of Edward (or, more precisely, of the flamboyant car he's driving). Before Vivian knows anything about Edward—before she even knows what he looks like—she spots his car, exclaiming to Kit, "That's a Lotus Esprit!" We learn moments later that she knows a lot about cars, but at this point, her excitement underscores the difference between the poverty-stricken life she leads and the preposterously wealthy one that Edward takes for granted.

In many of the movie's subsequent scenes, this theme of social inequality fades to the background. But it's never entirely absent from the narrative. Quite the contrary, it's the ingredient that creates the tension between Edward and Vivian that is necessary for sustaining the viewer's interest in their romance; like *West Side Story* (1961), *Pretty Woman* uses social inequality to raise the stakes of its romance plot. Of course, as is the way of romantic comedies, this inequality—and the clash of worldviews that it generates—finds its resolution in the final kiss that signals the beginning of the (wealthy) happily ever after. But until the movie's final minutes, it's a major element of the narrative.

The contradictions of money ("We both screw people for money")

Like the rest of *Pretty Woman*'s plot, the initial dialogue between Edward and Vivian revolves around money. Edward stops on Hollywood Boulevard because he's lost (and unable to get Phil's car into first gear). Vivian approaches him in the hope of earning back the rent money Kit has spent. When it turns out that Edward only wants directions, she tells him that these cost five dollars. When he scoffs at the ridiculousness of her request, she responds, "Price just went up to ten." When he asks for change for a twenty, she hops in his car and says, "For twenty, I'll show you personal."

Later in the same scene, Vivian states, "I never joke about money." "Neither do I," he responds. In this manner, the movie emphasizes that even though Vivian and Edward live in two very different worlds, both of these worlds are centered on money. This is one way in which the original script's commentary regarding the parallels between prostitution and corporate raiding persists in the romcom version. As Edward succinctly states after their dinner with Mr. Morse, "You and I are such similar creatures, Vivian. We both screw people for money."

On some level, this statement sets the foundation for the romance to come by communicating that Edward and Vivian share a fundamental attitude that allows them to understand each other's motivations: in a weirdly roundabout—decidedly unromantic—manner, it suggests that Edward and Vivian are kindred spirits (and perhaps even soul mates). Yet it also illustrates the ambivalence toward money that I started to comment on when I said that I disagree with critics who accuse the movie of openly promoting an ethos of capitalist greed and conspicuous consumption. I don't think that viewers are meant to relish Edward's statement as a model for how the good life is to be lived. Rather, the statement invites us to condemn it. This, in part, is what I meant when I said that *Pretty Woman*'s message about money is mixed in the sense that it manages to be critical of the very affluence that it simultaneously allows the viewer to vicariously experience.

This theme is worth exploring in greater detail. Let me start with the more obvious side of the coin, namely that the movie offers a neoliberal emphasis on the effort it takes to become wealthy as well as on the advantages that affluence brings. For starters, Edward is presented as a hardworking businessman. Likewise, Vivian—and this may be less evident—is presented as a striver: despite her profession, she's portrayed as a neoliberal subject who takes responsibility for herself and is willing to work for her success and (eventual) happiness. The opening scenes draw a contrast between Vivian and Kit precisely by depicting Vivian as the responsible one: the one who worries about paying rent while Kit squanders their money on drugs. This is how the movie instantly conveys that Vivian is not really "meant" to be a prostitute.

Vivian is new in town and squeaky clean whereas Kit—though a likable character—has been practicing the trade for a while. Kit is not as far gone as the dead prostitute in the dumpster who is described as "trading her sorry self for some crack." But compared to Vivian, Kit is hardened and (perhaps?) beyond repair. When Vivian asks her, "Don't you want to get out of here?," she responds, "Out of where? Where the fuck you want to go?" At the end, the movie also establishes Kit as a neoliberal striver by giving her a final dialogue about a beauty course she's "looking into." "You just can't turn tricks forever. You gotta have a goal," Kit concludes, thereby entering the neoliberal world of legitimate pursuits. But her fate remains uncertain whereas the audience knows from the movie's first few minutes that Vivian will be rewarded for her efforts.

In this manner, *Pretty Woman* advocates the neoliberal script of self-improvement, including the idea that anyone can make it if she just tries hard enough (a theme I'll return to below). Though Vivian stumbles at the beginning (another theme I'll return to below), by the end of the movie, she has proven herself to be a savvy business woman—one who is able to translate a blowjob into a marriage proposal—so that it's her acumen as an "entrepreneur," as a neoliberal go-getter, rather than merely her distinction as a "pretty woman" that wins her the jackpot.

On the "pro-money" side of *Pretty Woman*, we also find the relentless consumption that early critics found so distasteful. This is a common dimension of romantic comedies, which tend to offer an array of luxury items—particularly clothes, shoes, jewelry, and accessories—for spectators to admire. The so-called fashion movie, such as *The Devil Wears Prada* and *Sex and the City: The Movie*, in fact often foregrounds the display of such items over other plot elements to such a degree that the details of the story matter much less than the sumptuousness of commercial surfaces.[26] Extravagant settings are important in such movies as well, which invariably provide a parade of posh parties, hotels, restaurants, bars, and domestic settings. The same trend is noticeable in popular television shows centered on the lifestyle of the über-rich, such as *Gossip Girl*.

Pretty Woman is no exception to this trend. Much of it is set in the luxurious Regent Beverly Wilshire and other opulent settings such as expensive stores, the Voltaire, the San Francisco Opera, an elegant polo match, and—of course—limousines. The breakfast spread that meets Vivian her first morning in Edward's hotel suite is the epitome of excess: Edward has ordered every item on the breakfast menu because he doesn't know what she likes (incidentally, *Gossip Girl* frequently displays copious amounts of beautifully laid out food that none of the super-thin characters have time to eat). And then there are the clothes: dresses, suits, hats, shoes, stockings, and other accessories. There is therefore no way to deny that *Pretty Woman* relishes the pleasures of consumption, creating a kind of "shop window" for viewers.[27]

But the other side of the coin is that the movie also denounces the lifestyle of the unreasonably rich. This is why I want to counter Greenberg's assessment that *Pretty Woman* caters to the tastes of "the unrepentantly wealthy"[28] by pointing out that, quite the contrary, it consistently depicts the moneyed class (beyond Edward) as arrogant, shallow, and corrupt. This is particularly obvious at the polo match where Phil, having learned from Edward that Vivian is a hooker, propositions her. This is moments after a high-society lady has called her Edward's "flavor of the month." "Are these people your friends?" Vivian incredulously asks Edward, suggesting that, for all their money, the people Edward associates with are callous scoundrels. This is why I would say, contra Smith, that Vivian's "peasant manners" pale in comparison to the crassness of *Pretty Woman*'s rich people. In addition, that the movie portrays its archetypal corporate raider, Phil, as a sleazy wannabe-rapist seems like a pointed statement about the corroding influence of money.

Phil is, throughout the movie, presented as the greedier, more ruthless version of Edward, as, for instance, when he asks Edward (in reference to Mr. Morse), "We have his nuts on the block. What are you waiting for?" When Edward decides to join forces with Mr. Morse instead of destroying his company, Phil takes his fury out on Vivian by forcing himself on her, screaming "Is this 20 bucks? 30 Bucks? You a fifty-dollar whore?" For all of Vivian's faux pas with high-society manners, the final message of the movie is that it's Phil—the guy who places money above all else—who lacks not only manners but also a moral compass. In this way, the movie walks a tightrope between, on the one hand, offering us atrocious rich people we love to hate and, on the other, promoting the neoliberal creed of effort leading to success. Or to approach the matter from the opposite direction, it allows us to indulge in the fantasy of bottomless wealth at the same time as it invites us to recoil from the vulgarity of some of the people who get to live out this fantasy.

As *Pretty Woman*'s plot progresses, it becomes clear that, besides Edward and Mr. Morse, there are absolutely no decent rich people in the movie. In contrast, Vivian's world, while rough, contains elements of warmth and loyalty, as exemplified by the friendship between Vivian and Kit. The latter is a common element of romantic comedies, which tend to insist on solidarity between women even if they also often present women as competing with each other or being mean to each other (as the Rodeo Drive sales women are to Vivian). As Hilary Radner states, "Women who fail to understand their connection to other women will not enjoy success or happiness within the world of the girly film."[29] Such films, Radner specifies, are premised on the idea that female friends will always have each other's backs. This is the case in *Pretty Woman*, where Vivian and Kit repeatedly tell each other to "take care of you." The contrast of this solidarity to how most of the rich people in the movie treat each other—and Vivian—adds yet another layer to its critique of wealth.

The heartlessness of Edward's wealthy world sets the stage for Edward to be rescued by Vivian just as much as Vivian is rescued by Edward. I'll return to this central component of the movie later in my analysis. At this juncture, I merely want to stress that the last line Vivian speaks—"she rescues him right back"—alludes to something that has already happened within the movie's narrative: by the time Edward "rescues" Vivian from poverty, she has rescued him from the barrenness of his affluent existence by humanizing him, by showing him how to love, and by teaching him to enjoy life's little pleasures.

It's unfortunate that this is the kind of rescue that women have throughout the ages been expected to offer men: as I noted in the previous chapter, in the gender order of yesteryear, the man was supposed to make a living whereas the woman was supposed to alleviate the harshness of the effort that making a good living entails; she was supposed to make his life bearable, which—as we know before we even meet Vivian—is exactly what Vivian will do for Edward. In this regard, *Pretty Woman* is terribly retrograde.

But I think that it's also important to note the significance of the fact that it's specifically the cold comforts of excessive wealth that Vivian rescues Edward from. When Edward gets lost in Hollywood, he's already emotionally "lost," unable to find his way to a rewarding life. This is one way in which the movie imparts the idea that money alone cannot satisfy. It implies that something more enlivening than money is needed to attain a genuinely good life. Vivian's role is to provide this vitalizing touch to Edward's wooden character. If in Ovid's story, Pygmalion brings Galatea to life through his touch, in *Pretty Woman*, it's Vivian who brings Edward to life through her touch. Vivian may be transformed by a new wardrobe, by Edward's high-class stylistic preferences and robust bank account, but Edward's transformation is much more profound, impacting the very depths of his character.

The racial politics of class mobility ("You clean up real nice")

In the pages that follow, I'll return to Edward's transformation, for I think that it's one of the main reasons that many viewers with feminist sensibilities were, and still are, willing to tolerate Vivian's transformation rather than censor it as blatantly antifeminist. But first I want to look at the racial politics of *Pretty Woman*'s Cinderella fantasy. Like all versions of this fantasy, *Pretty Woman* is a story about class mobility: the visual transformation of Vivian from a hooker to a lady—and the movie's emphasis is strongly on the word *lady*—signifies her ascent on the socioeconomic ladder. This ascent, in turn, presupposes whiteness. As Madison observes, even though the movie ostensibly offers a "universal" story of class mobility, its plot can only unfold in the manner it does because Vivian is a pretty woman who also happens to be white. Madison adds, "One need only mentally substitute a beautiful black woman in Vivian's role to understand how thoroughly racial difference and its absence informs this contemporary fairy tale."[30]

Madison here foregrounds Toni Morrison's insight that, within American culture, even when race isn't explicitly part of a narrative, its "shadow hovers in implication, in sign, in line or demarcation."[31] Race, in other words, is never absent conceptually even when it's absent visually or rhetorically; even when a story isn't "about" race, it's about race. This is why Madison argues that, from the perspective of the black feminist spectator, "When Edward meets Vivian, a Pandora's box of gender, racial, and economic implications relative to power issues is opened."[32] Even something as basic as Vivian's ability to stay at the Regent after her first night with Edward is arguably premised on her whiteness, on her ability to begin to blend in with the rest of the hotel's guests.

Although I suggested above that the demand that a romcom like *Pretty Woman* show life as "it really is," let alone engage in a profound social commentary, is unreasonable, I agree with Madison that it's important to remain aware of the racial and class-related messages of the film. When it comes to the intersection of race and class specifically, retaining a degree of critical distance from the movie's narrative denaturalizes the movie's implicit claims to universality. As Madison puts it, "The prince and the princess . . . 'look' and 'act' and 'desire' according to specific norms—they are always white or nubile or beautiful (most often all three)."[33]

Madison suggests that being a "pretty" woman in the sense that *Pretty Woman* means the term can only become a reality for a white woman. There are some exceptions to the rule: when Kevin Costner cast Whitney Houston in the role of the female lead in *The Bodyguard* (1992), he caused a stir, as people speculated that the movie's romance wouldn't work.[34] But it sort of did, not the least because audiences flocked to the theaters to witness an interracial romance, and also perhaps because Houston was already an immensely successful singer. One can well imagine a contemporary romantic comedy with Beyoncé as the leading lady. Famous actors of any color would probably line up to play Romeo to her Juliet. But the norm has traditionally been that only white women can win the hearts of billionaires on the big screen.

That the norm doesn't represent everyone doesn't mean that those excluded by it can easily resist its allure. Instead, as Madison asserts, "Those outside the norm internalize the myth of the happy endings, as well as the stigma that, while they must live the myth to be happy and fulfilled, they do not meet the criteria of the myth."[35] That is, even those who are by definition marginalized by a given social myth frequently find the myth compelling while at the same time being aware of the various ways in which they fall short of its standards; those rejected by a cultural ideal may not be able to reject it in turn, unless, of course, they're politicized enough to have developed the oppositional gaze—analyzed by bell hooks—that I referred to in the last chapter. According to this interpretation, in the same way those in the throes of cruel optimism condone, and sometimes even celebrate, values that oppress them, women who are explicitly excluded from the happiness script of wealth through marriage can still take pleasure in watching this script unfold.

Although I appreciate the main outlines of Madison's interpretation, I want to put some pressure on it by noting that it comes uncomfortably close to Greenberg's statement—quoted earlier—about the false consciousness of women who, "knowing that they should know better," still guiltily enjoyed *Pretty Woman*. Should black women know even better than white women that they shouldn't enjoy *Pretty Woman*? Can we ask the viewer's desire—or the complex engagement with the movie narrative that this desire activates—to stay within the bounds of either race, class, gender, or sexual orientation?

Personally—and here I return to an example regarding the fluidity of spectator identification that I used in the previous chapter—I constantly insert myself into the fantasy worlds of male action heroes (of all colors): for the duration of the movie, I want exactly what they want, which is, invariably, to beat the bad guys. Likewise, I can easily name several lesbian friends of mine who, by their own admission, are "suckers" for straight romcoms. I'm not certain that such "unrealistic" identifications should be subjected to a straightforward politicization. It's not like watching a straight romcom causes my lesbian friends to want to marry Ashton Kutcher. And it's not like watching an action movie causes me to think that I can, in real life, leap from one tall building to another.

Still, it's useful to remain cognizant of the ways in which racial politics are built into the fabric of *Pretty Woman*. Because the movie's plot revolves so explicitly around money, its class politics are virtually impossible to miss. In contrast, the theme of race isn't emphasized, remaining for the most part the absent presence that Morrison describes, with the consequence that it's easy to overlook. Yet a closer inspection reveals that the movie's class politics are also, in many ways, the politics of race (and vice versa).

Pretty Woman uses racialization to establish its central class distinction between the haves and the have-nots. The party Edward leaves behind when he "descends" into the grime of Hollywood Boulevard is lily-white whereas Vivian's slice of Hollywood Boulevard is overtly coded as multiethnic. Scenes from the boulevard show a black man in Jamaican attire shouting the movie's key message—which I'll return to at the end of this chapter—of Hollywood being a place of dreams; two prostitutes—one black, one white—offering themselves to men passing by in cars; and drugs being transferred from white hands to black ones. When Vivian evades her landlord by climbing down her fire escape—in this way foreshadowing the movie's final scene in which Edward climbs up the same fire escape—we're shown a black woman eating a banana in one of the windows she passes. When we first meet Kit, she's hanging out with Carlos—a threatening Latino pimp—and two white women. Kit herself is coded as vaguely "ethnic" by her Italian last name (De Luca) and working-class accent. And a muscular black baseball player on a poster overlooks Hollywood.

The overall message of these plot elements and visual backdrops isn't necessarily that non-whites are always the lower classes: there are enough white people on Hollywood Boulevard to prevent this reading (and baseball players who are famous enough to get their picture printed on big-city posters make a ton of money). Rather, the message is that there is something chaotic, even potentially dangerous about the mixing of the races.

When Vivian leaves behind Hollywood Boulevard, she also leaves behind a multiracial world, inserting herself into Edward's all-white environment. Furthermore, one could argue that Vivian's image as "a 'good' bad girl"—as Madison calls her[36]—is carved against the bodies of racialized women, including Kit, who are portrayed as the "actual" hookers; the notion that Vivian isn't meant for a life of prostitution on Hollywood Boulevard is conveyed via a contrast with women who (more "naturally"?) are. When Kit says to Vivian after her transformation, "You clean up real nice," it's hard not to read racial difference into the statement: the implication is that, as a white woman, Vivian has the kinds of opportunities that Kit herself doesn't have.

The movie underscores this point by offering a host of marginal characters whose role it is to provide services to its rich white people: the Chinese men valet parking cars at Phil's party; Darryl, Edward's black limo driver who rescues him from the violence of Carlos's gang by revealing that he's carrying a gun (isn't every black man?); Mr. Thompson, whose ethnic identity (and sexual orientation) remains decidedly ambiguous; and some of the staff at the Regent, which is filled with white—and some Japanese—guests. This detail—that some of the guests at this luxury hotel are Japanese—is also interesting because it plays on a familiar racist trope: that of the hardworking, overachieving Japanese population that threatens to overtake white America. That the only nonwhite guests at the Regent are Japanese implies that if you follow the neoliberal creed of making an effort—as the Japanese, according to the American cultural imagination, do to an almost disturbing extent—you'll have money, and that money, if you have enough of it, allows you to transcend even the obstacle of racism.

The defiant cinderella
("I can do anything I want to, baby")

Pretty Woman's gender politics, like its class politics, are much more overtly on the surface than its racial politics. If it's a movie about money, it's also definitely a movie about gender. On some level, it may even be a movie about feminism: although it doesn't explicitly mention feminism, as *Miss Congeniality* does, it's in constant dialogue with feminism's popularized versions. Most obviously, it offers us a spunky heroine who, initially at least, refuses to adhere to the expected codes of feminine behavior.

Vivian may be on a low socioeconomic rung, but she's no pushover. Though there are scenes—such the one where Phil tries to rape her—where Vivian is shown to be timid, for the most part she's assertive and outspoken. Indeed, when reading Smith's assessment of her as "weak, dependent, and essentially helpless," and Greenberg's assessment of her as an "icon of passivity," I had to ask myself whether I had watched the same movie as these (male) critics, for Vivian, to me, appears anything but subservient or powerless.

It seems to me that the only thing Vivian lacks confidence in is her ability to shop—a point I'll return to below. Of course she also needs help with manners and salad forks, but these are entirely superficial aspects of the movie's social mobility theme. They don't say anything about Vivian's basic character, which *Pretty Woman* consistently portrays as tough, capable, and—as I stressed earlier—determined to succeed.

Vivian's independence is established early in the plot, during her initial dialogue with Edward, when she responds to his exasperated claim that she can't charge for directions with a defiant "I can do anything I want to, baby." Later in the movie, she responds to his request that they meet in the hotel lobby by saying, "I'll meet you in the lobby, but only 'cause you're paying me to." "We say who, we say when, we say how much" is her insubordinate response to Carlos pressuring her to have a pimp. Later, she repeats the same line to Edward in a slightly altered form: "You don't own me. I decide. I say who, I say when, I say who!" Edward may be paying Vivian for sex, but she's asserting her right to set the terms. Far from being an example of compliant traditional femininity, she exhibits the traits that Sherman (see Chapter 1) associates with active neoliberal femininity, including sexual agency.

Much of *Pretty Woman*'s comedy arises from the fact that Vivian openly ridicules Edward's upper-crust pretensions. For instance, when she first enters the Regent—wearing Edward's overcoat over her skimpy hooker outfit—she mocks his wishes to stay discreet by letting the coat open in order to taunt the scandalized hotel guests. When Edward and Vivian wait for the hotel elevator with a stiff middle-aged couple who give her disapproving looks, she lifts her leg on a trash can, hikes up her miniscule skirt, and says to Edward, "Oh, honey. You know what's happened? I've got a runner in my pantyhose." She then looks at the couple, laughs, and adds, "I'm not wearing pantyhose." When the elevator doors open, she marches in and blurts out, "Well, color me happy. There's a sofa in here for two." Striking a rebelliously sexual pose on the sofa, she stares at the appalled couple with mischievous amusement.

When Edward enters the elevator, Vivian states with obvious irony, "Sorry, couldn't help it." "Try," he dryly responds, but it's clear that she won't always do his bidding. Later—when they're about to enter the store on Rodeo Drive that will become the setting for her (second, successful) shopping spree—he asks her to get rid of her gum. To Edward's consternation, she spits it at two women passing by. Even the height of her performance as a "lady," her visit to the opera, is enlivened by her playful act of telling an elderly woman that she liked *La Traviata* so much that she almost peed her pants.

Smith dismisses these moments as bad screenwriting—suggesting that a man like Edward would never fall in love with a woman with such bad manners—but he doesn't take into account the immense satisfaction that such minor acts of social defiance can give to female viewers tired of being told to act like a lady. The lines I've just quoted are among the ones that women I talked to during the process of writing this book—many of whom had not seen the movie since it was released—cited with evident relish. A couple of these woman reminded me that in 1990 the only way to see a movie more than once was to keep paying the entrance fee to—yes!—an actual movie theater. This is exactly what they had done, until they had memorized their favorite lines. An 84-year-old woman, who has by all accounts spent much of her life acting like a lady, told me that she loved *Pretty Woman* because "Vivian is so naughty." She added that she particularly liked the snail scene.

Pretty Woman offers the delicious spectacle of a woman misbehaving. Furthermore, as the elevator scene illustrates, much of Vivian's irreverent behavior is linked to her sexual assertiveness. Early critics may have bemoaned the film's uncritical portrayal of prostitution, but female viewers who were used to seeing bashful heroines may have relished seeing a leading lady who plays a sexually knowledgeable prostitute.

This Cinderella doesn't meet her prince at a ball but on Hollywood Boulevard. Their first dialogue involves her informing him that she always uses condoms, gets herself checked once a month at a free clinic, and is better in the sack than an amateur. This is right before she reaches between his legs to check his penis for stiffness, announcing that it has "potential," and just about an hour (in narrative time) before she gives him a blowjob. Besides the crass talk about money, *Pretty Woman* offers a surprising amount—for a romantic comedy—of sexual frankness. This frankness obviously worked with female audiences. As I mentioned at the end of the previous chapter, the line Kit addresses to an elderly couple scandalized by her "slutty" wardrobe at the Regent—"Fifty bucks, grandpa. For seventy-five, the wife can watch"—has lingered with many women as a romcom line worth citing a quarter of a century later.

When male critics such as Smith and Greenberg moralize about *Pretty Woman*'s unrealistic depiction of prostitution,

I can't help but wonder whether what ultimately bothers them is the movie's portrayal of women as sexual initiators. Female viewers, in contrast, may have been ready for this portrayal; some of them may have been extremely tired of being told that good girls don't. Enter Julia Roberts—a good girl if there ever was one—doing it without apology. Many of the critics I quoted at the beginning of this chapter are feminist enough to recognize that the movie's marriage plot is far from being progressive but they're not feminist enough—or not feminist in the right way— to recognize that the female sexual assertiveness that the movie also showcases can be read as a feminist statement.

Isn't there something rather brazen about a fairytale where the heroine's first sexual encounter with the prince is not a kiss but a blowjob? This is one version of feminism. It's certainly not the only one, and perhaps not the one that the general public is most familiar with. And as I argued in the last chapter, by now the sexually assertive woman has become a truism of yawn-inducing proportions. But in 1990, such a woman was still an innovation, at least in the world of romantic comedies and other movies aimed at women specifically.

Softening the gender binary ("Standard H? Like I know what that means")

Another way in which *Pretty Woman* caters to feminist sensibilities is its consistent attempt to soften the rigidly dichotomous paradigms of gender that our society has for so long taken for granted. This is nowhere more apparent than in the opening sequence, which erodes these paradigms by illustrating that Vivian is a much better driver than Edward. Hollywood movies often look for concise ways of conveying a great deal of meaning in a short span of time (so as to get going with the main narrative). When it comes to meddling with normative notions of gender difference, driving offers an effective shorthand of this kind. I would in fact say that the early exchange between Edward and Vivian about driving that takes place in the Lotus Esprit is essential for setting the tone of the entire movie as well as for guaranteeing that female spectators don't walk out of the theater disgusted by yet another display of how a woman is fashioned by a man.

That Edward isn't good at driving a stick shift is an aspect of his characterization that instantly establishes him as a likable character: he's not a macho caricature but a guy who can get a little flustered. Equally importantly, this scene allows the movie to emphasize that Vivian is not a fluffy girly-girl, thereby ensuring that later scenes in the movie—such as the shopping spree—that risk giving us the impression that she's stuck in a prefeminist femininity don't define her character.

Arguably, Vivian's character is defined irreversibly during the early scene in the car. Here is the relevant dialogue, beginning with Vivian's admiration for the Lotus Esprit:

Vivian: Man, this baby must corner like it's on rails.
Edward: Beg your pardon?
Vivian: Doesn't it blow your mind? This is only four cylinders.
Edward: You know about cars. Where did that come from?
Vivian: *Road & Track*. Boys back home I grew up with were really into American heavy metal: Mustangs, Corvettes. They bought 'em cheap, fixed them up. I paid attention.

Vivian pauses and then adds in a mocking tone of voice:

So, how is it you know so little about cars?
Edward: My first car was a limousine. So, where is this heavy metal home?

Edward shifts gears badly (as he has throughout the opening scenes); the transmission screeches

Vivian: Milledgeville, Georgia. . . . You know, I think you left your transmission back there. You're not shifting right. This is a standard H.

Edward: Standard H? Like I know what that means. You ever driven a Lotus?
Vivian (*wishfully*): No.
Edward: You're gonna start right now.
Vivian: You're joking (*laughing*).
Edward: No, it's the only way I can get you off my coat.

They switch seats.

Vivian: Fasten your seat belt. I'm taking you for the ride of your life. I'm gonna show you what this car can really do. Are you ready?
Edward: I am ready.
Vivian: Hang on.
Edward: Okay.
Vivian: Here we go.

Vivian drives fast and shifts flawlessly.

Vivian (*in a gently mocking tone*): This has pedals like a race car. They're really close together. So it's probably easier for a woman to drive 'cause they have little feet. Except me. I wear a size 9.

This bit of dialogue accomplishes a lot. Through a simple role reversal—humorously playing with one of the most persistent gender stereotypes of our culture, namely that women are bad drivers—it renders the movie's eventual slide into more normative gender roles more palatable, taking the sting out of what could otherwise be seen as dreadfully retrograde plot. Not only does it highlight Vivian's expertise with cars but it also reveals that Edward is able to take a joke, that he's not threatened by Vivian's competence. "Standard H? Like I know what that means" achieves two aims: it highlights Edward's privilege—that he's used to being driven around—and it illustrates that he's not a sexist jerk who feels the need to put women down when they encroach on "his" territory.

That this gender reversal entails driving is simple but powerful. I thought of this recently when driving a male friend in hectic Boston traffic: notoriously a demanding driving situation. Out of the blue, my passenger said, "You're a pretty good driver. You're definitely better than my mother." If I hadn't had to watch the traffic, I would have smacked him—hard. Just a few months earlier I had been in a car with him when he almost ran over a woman pushing a baby stroller on a crosswalk. Driving is an activity where masculine arrogance routinely flares up, even in guys who are otherwise egalitarian. This is why *Pretty Woman*'s driving sequence is so effective in setting the movie's tone as nonsexist (a detail, perhaps unsurprisingly, lost on the male critics who accused it of outrageous sexism).

Vivian even mocks the all-too-common phenomenon of women trying to play down their skills in order to compensate for usurping masculine prerogative. When she specifies that the pedals of the Lotus are close together, therefore "probably" making it easier for a woman to drive it, she's saying what a woman might say to a man to make him feel better about not being as good at something as she is. But her sardonic tone makes it impossible to take her seriously—and the look on Edward's face reveals that he doesn't. He knows—and admits—that he sucks at driving and that the size of his feet has nothing to do it. I can see why female viewers would appreciate this, along with Vivian's revelation that she wears a size 9 shoe (though, admittedly, this can't quite make up for the fact that she wears what looks like a size 0 miniskirt).

Pretty Woman works hard to portray Edward as the very opposite of a condescending misogynist. He's polite, with a wry sense of humor. Consider, for instance, the scene in which Edward invites Vivian to his hotel suite:

Edward: I was thinking, did you really say $100 an hour?
Vivian: Yeah.
Edward: Well, if you don't have any prior engagements, I'd be very pleased if you'd accompany me into the hotel.
Vivian: You got it. What is your name?
Edward: Edward.

Vivian (*in a teasing voice*): Edward? That's my *favorite* name in the whole world.
Edward (*emulating incredulity*): No?
Vivian: I tell you what, this is fate, Edward. That's what this is.

This is what so many women appreciate about the heartthrobs of romantic comedies: the guys are decent, smart, witty, and amusing. Edward's invitation is almost comically courteous, given that, at this point in the plot, he's soliciting a prostitute. And he—once again—reveals that he can play into Vivian's humor in a slightly self-deprecating manner. In the same way that he accepted her jokes about his bad driving, he accepts her mockery of the expectation that, as a prostitute, she's going to flatter him in every possible way, starting with his name. Her teasing tone is meant to convey that she's not about to do this, even if her concluding "this is fate" already has a ring of sincerity to it. The witty banter—a common ingredient of romantic comedies—between Edward and Vivian is one of the movie's pleasures: she matches his intellect, visibly relishing the banter.

Rewriting the scripts of gender ("I'm just using him for sex")

Pretty Woman's attempt to soften—even deconstruct—the gender binary is the main way in which it anticipates third-wave feminism. Indeed, it engages in this attempt much more overtly than most recent romantic comedies, which are usually content to present a beautiful heroine who is good at her job without feeling the need to assert that she excels in areas of life that have traditionally been aligned with masculinity. By presenting Vivian as a car-loving, penis-grabbing gal who isn't afraid to speak her mind, the movie hits some important third-wave feminist notes at the same time as it promotes the second-wave feminist theme of the basic equality of men and women. Yet it also manages to cater to postfeminist inclinations with its "girly" aspects, such as the shopping scene. No wonder, then, that it charmed so many different types of female viewers.

I've already called attention to Vivian's sexual assertiveness. This is one of *Pretty Woman*'s most obvious ways of rewriting the scripts of gender. When Vivian tells two stuck-up women at the polo match that she's not trying to "land" Edward—as the women assume—but "just using him for sex," she demolishes the idea that women only want sex in the context of serious relationships. Likewise, when she reveals to Edward that when she's with a client, she acts like an emotionally detached "robot," she undermines the notion that women's sexuality is indissociable from love. Even the fact that she and Edward end up "in love" cannot quite erase the impact of these statements, for the combination of these plot elements conveys that Edward is "modern" enough to not be turned off by a woman who knows how to separate sex and love.

At the same time, *Pretty Woman* finds various ways to present Edward as emotionally vulnerable. For example, we learn that he has spent years in therapy trying to get over the fact that his father left his mother for another woman when he was a boy. Indeed, we discover that his ruthless business practice of destroying companies arises from his anger toward his father, whose company he acquired early in his career as revenge for this abandonment. In this way, Edward's corporate brutality is mitigated—given a "reason"—by the revelation of his father's painful act of betrayal (while Edward is shown to be loyal to his mother). This is a transparent attempt to render him likable.

Like every romantic comedy, *Pretty Woman* needs to create a leading man who is strong but also a little wounded, confident but also sensitive and considerate. The effect of this is automatically to erase some of the differences between men and women that our culture has historically insisted on. This explains why romcoms, which may otherwise be fairly conformist, tend to be pioneering on gender, offering us women who don't act quite the way that women have traditionally been expected to act and men who don't act quite the way that men have traditionally been expected to act.

There are those who ridicule this aspect of romcoms, accusing them of nurturing fantasmatic depictions of gentle men and egalitarian gender relations that contradict the harsh realities of today's gender politics. Such depictions of gender-bending, we're told, are mere wish-fulfillments, lulling women into complacency about the triumphs of feminism. Yet one could just as easily argue that romcoms present a utopian vision of what women, particularly feminists, would like to see take place in the real world, that—whether they so intend or not—they often uphold the ideals of the kind of (third-wave) feminism that wants to defeat gendered thinking and the inequalities that such thinking supports.

I've emphasized that the persistence of active gender stereotyping—the stubborn adherence to a strictly binaristic model of gender—is part of our culture's backlash against feminist victories. As a matter of fact, it seems to me that the more equal men and women become, the more relentlessly some of our cultural authorities strive to convince us that a gender-bifurcated world is what we should all want—that, indeed, it's the only *natural* order of things, so that every attempt to create a more egalitarian system represents a breach of the laws of nature. Against this backdrop, romantic comedies could be argued to be a resistant form of entertainment, for they tend to counter the mentality of gender stereotyping by offering us men and women who are attractive in part because they don't adhere to normative codes of gender.

Moreover, to the degree that romcoms aren't invested in traditional gender roles, they also aren't interested in preserving the Great Divide—the battle of the sexes—between men and women. This isn't to say that romantic comedies aren't filled with masculine men and feminine women. But their masculinity and femininity is usually undercut by characteristics that align them with the "opposite" sex, so that one could say that a degree of androgyny is the ideal of romantic comedies.

The female pygmalion
("She rescues him right back")

Given that the third-wave feminist focus on deconstructing the gender binary only gained prominence during the decades after the release of *Pretty Woman*, it's understandable that the movie's early critics ignored this aspect of its fantasy world, that they, in some ways, looked for feminism in the wrong places. The lens of third-wave feminism also clarifies why Edward's transformation is just as important—and perhaps even more so—as that of Vivian to *Pretty Woman*'s success as a modern fairytale. As I stressed earlier, the movie's main character arc belongs to Edward rather than to Vivian: she may undergo a superficial makeover of attire and manners but he undergoes a fundamental "makeover" of character.

Edward's makeover is accomplished through the subplot of him changing his mind about taking over Mr. Morse's company. Due to Vivian's influence, Edward realizes that he wants to build things rather than to destroy them (though it's of course ironic that what he intends to build with Mr. Morse are navy destroyers). One can see how this supports the neoliberal script that valorizes productiveness: the building of things. One could also easily criticize the problematic nature of the message that it sends about capitalism, namely that capitalism merely needs some civilizing—that, as a system, it's more or less okay as long as it's practiced in a principled way. But this is not the message that female viewers—who arguably don't watch romcoms for their commentary on economic systems—are likely to fixate on; rather, they're likely to focus on the theme of mutual rescue—the message of gender equality—that the movie aspires toward (even if it at times falters).

I've conceded that it's questionable that Vivian's rescue of Edward takes the conventional form of putting him in touch with his repressed emotions, that it's Vivian's "feminine" touch that turns Edward into a more humane capitalist, not to mention a more fully rounded person. Undoubtedly, Edward is initially depicted as a victim of his success, so that Vivian's task becomes to erase the callous side of this success by drawing him out of his emotional detachment, ruthless calculation, and unnecessary aggression. Though Edward is also seen to support Vivian emotionally—as is the case when he tells her that she's smarter than she thinks—it's Vivian who is the emotional center of the narrative, who is shown to transform Edward from a work-obsessed man haunted by the emptiness of his life to a man who knows how to take a day off.

Edward rescues Vivian financially; Vivian rescues Edward emotionally. As a result, *Pretty Woman* could be said to promote the heteropatriarchal fantasy that men and women have complementary roles to play in life—the fantasy that, as I've demonstrated, feeds the idea that heterosexual marriage is the only "natural" way to organize our private lives. Even Vivian's last name, Ward—which fits snugly into Edward's first name—suggests this reading. Yet the matter is complicated by the fact that in abandoning the barracuda tactics of his business practice, Edward leaves behind a hypermasculine world of cutthroat competition. He bows out of a version of masculinity that our society has traditionally rewarded and embraces a version of manhood that has, arguably, been touched by feminism.

On this view, the humanization of Edward is yet another way in which *Pretty Woman* advocates the third-wave feminist ideal of leveling distinctions between men and women. Moreover, that Vivian manages to transform Edward—and that his transformation is arguably more drastic than hers—contributes to the sense that an equal exchange of some kind has taken place between these characters; it ensures that, within the movie's narrative logic, Vivian's final words—"she rescues him right back"—ring true. This is why I argued earlier that Vivian is better read as Pygmalion than Galatea. From the beginning of the movie, Vivian is portrayed as a vivacious, dynamic character who offers a clear contrast to Edward's subdued—almost numb—personality. As the plot progresses, we witness his emotional awakening. He may be the Pygmalion of the story in terms of molding Vivian's appearance, but she's the Pygmalion of the story in terms of animating Edward, therefore reworking the foundations of his character.

The masquerade of femininity ("No one can look as good as you")

This far in my analysis, I've attempted to show that *Pretty Woman*'s messages about money and gender are more complicated than many early critics assumed. It's now time to tackle the aspect of the movie that is most difficult—perhaps impossible—to reconcile with feminism, unless one understands feminism to be a vehicle for neoliberal femininity as a commercial construct. As we've learned, for many postfeminist women, female empowerment has indeed been reduced to the right to shop. That *Pretty Woman* contributes to this mentality is obvious, for Vivian's climb up the social ladder is accomplished largely through her physical makeover. One could even argue that the movie works so hard in the opening scenes to present Vivian as an independent heroine because it needs to neutralize the potentially offensive aspects of the makeover plot to come, because it needs some way of making sure that we don't squirm in our seats in the way we do when we watch Judy's transformation in *Vertigo*.

This is a common strategy in makeover movies: *She's All That* (1999), *Miss Congeniality* (2000), *The Princess Diaries* (2001), *A Cinderella Story* (2004), and *Pitch Perfect* (2012), for instance, all present the same storyline of an independent, spirited young woman who is a bit rough around the edges but who happens to stumble into a situation in which she must be made over to look like a beauty pageant contestant, princess, lead singer, or (at least) a superhot date. These movies also invariably replicate the original Cinderella's status as an underdog who must fight her way into success.

Pretty Woman presents the quintessential underdog: a poverty-stricken prostitute. The later examples offer a variation on the theme by portraying female protagonists who aren't necessarily mopping the floors—though this is exactly what Hilary Duff does at the beginning of *A Cinderella Story*—but who have for one reason or another fallen into the role of the socially disparaged ugly duckling. This underdog status is central to all of the movies in question, for there is perhaps no other theme more guaranteed to thrill American audiences than the rise of the downtrodden.

We see this theme in action movies where the hero starts out outnumbered by the enemy (but in the end slays them all). We see it in detective stories where the male lead starts out as a divorced alcoholic who has trouble getting out of bed (but in the end solves his case). We see it in thrillers where the protagonist can't initially convince anyone, and especially her boss, that there is a plot to bomb America, an outbreak of a deadly virus, or a volcano about to erupt (but in the end saves the day). We see it in sports movies where the rookie can't score a goal even when the field is wide open (but in the end brings the team to victory). And we see it in romantic comedies where the heroine starts out as an ugly duckling with bushy eyebrows, baggy sweaters, and eye-glasses from the 1980s. And then we watch her rise. What could be more satisfying?

The masquerade of femininity is how the ugly duckling of romantic comedies rises. This is even more the case in romantic comedies that are also makeover movies, as *Pretty Woman* is. If *Pretty Woman*, generally speaking, is about money and gender, the masquerade of femininity, including the commercial aspects of this masquerade, is its most important subplot. You'll recall that Joan Riviere argued that women often resort to the masquerade of femininity in order to preempt male punishment for their competence. But Riviere already suggested that, in the final analysis, there isn't much of a difference between the masquerade of femininity and femininity as such. This is what third-wave feminist analyses of gender also imply. Notably, it's the message of *Pretty Woman* as well. As a matter of fact, if one were to look for a way to turn *Pretty Woman*'s masquerade of femininity into a feminist theme—which I've admitted is a difficult task—one could argue that the movie foregrounds the constructed nature of femininity to such an extent that it becomes entirely denaturalized.

It's impossible to watch *Pretty Woman* without realizing that Judith Butler is correct in postulating that gender is a performative accomplishment. More specifically, it's impossible to avoid recognizing that becoming a woman who meets the beauty standards of our society takes an enormous amount of conscious exertion. *Pretty Woman*, like most makeover movies, communicates this—ultimately rather simple—message much more efficiently than the convoluted sentences of academic feminism. Indeed, we don't even need to wait until the makeover scene for the memo on this: the theme begins to unfold the moment Vivian is introduced in the opening sequence (the same sequence that shows Edward getting lost in Phil's car).

In this sequence, Vivian is first shown waking up in her bed, the alarm alerting her to the fact that it's now late enough in the evening to begin her shift as a streetwalker. The first shot shows Vivian's buttocks in lacy black panties. The camera isolates this area of her body, so we have no choice but to admire the perfect form of her firm butt. She then turns around slowly, and the camera holds its focus, so we now have no choice but to admire her barely covered crotch. This is a fairly standard way of introducing a female character, so standard in fact that Sofia Coppola chooses to parody it in the opening shot of *Lost in Translation* (2011), which focuses on Scarlett Johansson's buttocks for so long that the viewer, presumably even one invested in the male gaze, starts to fidget, desperately looking for other objects for his gaze.

Pretty Woman isn't trying to comment on the stale trope of a woman's shapely ass, so the camera quickly pans up Vivian's body, revealing a red cropped top and a mass of red hair covered by a pillow. As Vivian's arm reaches for the alarm, the camera shifts to an array of photos stuck to the wall. On these—where we get our first glimpse of Vivian's face—she's shown wearing regular (even sloppy) clothes: jeans, t-shirt, sweatshirts, silly hats. She looks like the girl next door (a detail that tells us immediately that she's out of place on Hollywood Boulevard). The men whose arms are around her in the pictures have been visually mutilated in various ways: in the first, the photo is torn in such a way that the man's head is missing; in the second, the guy's face has been scratched off; in the third, the entire man has been edited out by ripping the photo in half, so that only Vivian is left standing. A space is therefore created for the arrival of Edward. We learn that, like Edward, Vivian hasn't had good relationships; she has still to find her one true love.

Next we see Vivian, now standing, start to dress for hooker-duty by lifting a white cropped top over her black bra. We still don't see her face so the photos remain our only clue to what she looks like above the shoulders. Instead a cut leads us to Edward's face, peering out of his car, noticeably lost. So we know that a meeting is inevitable. The only question is how it's going to happen. Back in Vivian's room, we watch her apply magic marker to her worn boot, the zipper of which is held up by a safety pin. But—because the masquerade of femininity is all about surface appearances—this doesn't stop her from looking appropriately alluring for streetwalking.

From beginning to end, the sequence that introduces Vivian's character—a sequence that, notably, is entirely visual, devoid of any dialogue or verbal explanation—gives us a close-up of what the masquerade of femininity, on a purely technical level, entails: choose the right clothes, mask all visible flaws, and flaunt the strengths (in this case, among many other things, long enough legs to carry off the high boots). Vivian crowns the performance with a glamorous blonde wig. When we finally see her face outside of the photos, she's applying mascara—an essential ingredients of the masquerade of femininity if there ever was one. Even the fact that the first shot of her face shows her looking in a mirror further accentuates the artifice that goes into the masquerade of femininity.

Significantly, the body we've been admiring up until the moment when Vivian's face is finally revealed in the mirror has been that of Julia Roberts's body double, Shelley Michelle. The uninformed viewer doesn't know this—the transitions are done seamlessly enough to preserve the illusion that we're watching Roberts's body—so the scene illustrates how movies manage to concoct a version of normative femininity that is more perfect than any one woman could ever accomplish on her own. In this forceful enactment of the masquerade of femininity, we get a composite product, one that combines the flawlessness of a carefully selected female body with the gorgeous face of an actress who is on her way to becoming one of Hollywood's most desirable stars.

Movies use body doubles to create icons of femininity that no one woman—not even Julia Roberts—can approximate on her own. Not only does she have a host of makeup artists, wardrobe designers, lighting experts, and editing professionals at her disposal, but she even has *another woman* to substitute for her whenever a scene calls for a well-formed butt. This is obviously the case in many other movies as well, so that the immaculate, even hyperbolic, femininity (and masculinity) of Hollywood stars is best understood as a performance that demands the labor of many. The practice of body doubling, then, gives us a very concrete way to understand what it means to engage in the masquerade of femininity in mainstream movies.

Roberts's body double also appears in the all-important shopping scene on Rodeo Drive. I'll return to other aspects of this scene momentarily. For now, let's note that the body that is shown trying on clothes in a dressing room is that of the double. In her interpretation of the significance of the double in *Pretty Woman*, Ann Chisholm argues that the visual effects of this scene and the opening sequence spill over to other scenes so that, throughout the movie, we read Robert's character as being partially constituted by her double.

According to Chisholm, even in scenes where the double is not used, her ghost haunts the imagery because we mentally keep substituting her body for the body of Roberts. Though we may not be consciously thinking of what Roberts's body looks like underneath her clothes, our assumption is that it looks like the body of the body double. This is why Chisholm writes:

> When Vivian (Julia Roberts) leaves the boutique in a new ensemble (the object of admiring glances from well-suited men as she walks down Rodeo Drive), and when she attends the polo match in one of the dresses modeled in the "fashion show" sequence, her screen presence and perceptions of her femininity are . . . the culmination of the prior substitution of another woman's body.[37]

Chisholm may be overstating the case, given that we see Roberts scantily clad throughout much of the first half of the movie. But her overall point is worth contemplating: in order to attain the textbook femininity that *Pretty Woman* demands, two women are needed. In this sense, as Chisholm notes, "The double is key to the film's mobilization of desire."[38] The double is essential for establishing Vivian as an object of desire—not just of the sexual desire of Edward but also of the identificatory desire of the straight female spectator.

Ironically—and it's not clear whether the irony is intentional or not—the dressing room scene is accompanied by Roy Orbison's lyrics: "I don't believe you, you're not the truth. . . . No one can look as good as you." We all know that the masquerade of femininity relies on illusion, that it's not "true," but we like to believe it anyway; we know that a woman that pretty must be a fantasy, but we like to look at her anyway. This is the power of fantasy—and the structure of fetishism, as I'll illustrate below.

From a hooker to a lady ("Either they love it or they hate it")

Although *Pretty Woman*'s shopping scene—the analysis of which I'll resume below—is perhaps the movie's most famous part, it's arguably not its most radical makeover scene. The latter may be when Vivian wakes up in Edward's suite after their first night together. Vivian walks out of the bedroom and finds Edward sitting in front of the enormous (and untouched) breakfast. Dressed in a luxurious hotel bathrobe, and without her blonde wig and lipstick, she looks like a completely different woman. Her long red hair provides a particularly striking contrast to her look of the previous night. We instantly realize that the hooker look was a performance (the *true* masquerade of femininity) and that we're now, supposedly, looking at the "real" woman, who, not incidentally, happens to be even more attractive than her hooker persona.

In the fantasy world of movies, the "real" woman often looks even better than her "made-up" version, in part because she's, of course, also "made up" by a makeup artist who has manipulated her look to be more "natural": what appears natural is merely a more muted version of made up. The lifting of the masquerade of femininity, in this sense, merely reveals a more subtle version of the masquerade. But within the movie narrative, we're looking at the woman as she, supposedly, "really is."

Pretty Woman underlines this sense of "realness" by depicting the Vivian of the morning after as much less brass and confident than her hooker incarnation the previous night. She approaches Edward's breakfast spread nervously, grabs a croissant, and saunters to the balcony, presumably to recollect herself. When she returns to the table, a conversation ensues in which Edward explains that he's about to buy Mr. Morse's company for the bargain price of a billion dollars. She chokes at the price and tentatively volunteers, "You must be really smart, huh? I only got through eleventh grade. How far did you go school?" When Edward responds that he went "all the way," she looks nervous—nervous in a way that is a far cry from her cheeky attitude of the night before.

We thus learn that, despite her lack of education and career accomplishments, Vivian is able to respect the "right" characteristics—characteristics that, as I explained in the previous chapter, underpin the individualistic neoliberal script of effort leading to a reward: ambition, talent, and hard work. When Vivian discovers that Edward has worked much of the night, she utters, "You don't sleep, you don't do drugs, you don't drink. You hardly eat. What do you do, Edward?" While her tone is slightly teasing, it's also admiring, signaling to the viewer that Edward's work ethic has impressed her.

The breakfast scene is crucial for understanding the makeovers to come: the black cocktail dress Vivian wears to the dinner with Mr. Morse, the polka-dot dress she wears to the polo match, the red gown she wears to the opera, and the casual but upscale outfits she wears when Edward finally—upon her urging—takes a day off and they wander around the city and go horseback riding. By giving us the "real" Vivian, a Vivian who doesn't look like a hooker, the breakfast scene illustrates that the makeovers to come do not transform Vivian into some other, artificial woman but merely make her a more sparkly version of who she *already is*. In other words, because we understand that the hooker look never reflected her genuine persona in the first place, we also understand that the new clothes she acquires do not violate this persona; quite the contrary, the new clothes give her a chance to become who she, in the "realness" of her being, is (or wants to be).

This is one reason that *Pretty Woman*'s shopping scene is not painful to watch in the same way as the shopping scene of *Vertigo* is: if Scottie forces Judy into a persona that has nothing to do with who she is and that she vehemently resists, Edward merely facilitates Vivian's transformation into the person that she, deep down, already is: she just needs the clothes to prove it. Though Vivian is being turned from a hooker to a lady, we recognize that she was much closer to a lady than to a hooker to begin with, that her hooker look was a disguise adopted due to dire circumstances. In the breakfast scene, she still exhibits some unladylike characteristics, such as chewing with her mouth open, but we're simultaneously being informed that this is a matter of upbringing—"I only got through eleventh grade"—rather than of lack of character, that ultimately she holds the same admirable values as Edward; we're being told that, at bottom, she's a noble creature, just like Edward, and therefore the woman he's meant to end up with.

Elizabeth Scala argues that it's the opera scene that most clearly illustrates Vivian's "intrinsic" nobility. In other words, Vivian's beautiful red gown and ruby necklace—which complete her transformation to a lady—merely reflect the beautiful soul that this scene unveils for the viewer's benefit. Edward sets the stage for this unveiling by telling Vivian before the opera begins that there are two kinds of people in the world: inspired ones who love opera and pedestrian ones who don't understand it. As he states, "People's reaction to opera the first time they see it is very dramatic. Either they love it or they hate it. If they love it, they will always love it. If they don't, they may learn to appreciate it, but it will never become part of their soul."

We therefore understand that Vivian is being tested. Edward wants to know which kind of person Vivian is, which is why he observes her face with intense attention throughout the performance. Predictably, she passes the test with flying colors, exhibiting all the emotional reactions he's hoping to see: she smiles and cries at the appropriate moments, revealing herself to be both pleased and moved. Scala explains that we get to witness "the music's unfalsifiable effect" on Vivian, her "spontaneous and therefore authentic reaction," a reaction that proves the equivalence between herself and Edward.[39] As Scala adds, "We might now conclude that opera has become part of Vivian's soul, as it is part of Edward's. This affinity will eventually, convention leads us to believe, allow Vivian to become part of Edward's soul because of this shared emotion."[40]

The opera scene thus confirms—in a more elevated setting—the kinship between Edward and Vivian that Edward already called attention to when he, earlier in the movie, said that they are similar creatures in the sense that they both screw people for money. The affinity between the hero and the heroine that the earlier scene—somewhat awkwardly for a romantic comedy—attempted to establish is confirmed in the opera scene. For Scala, this is one of the progressive aspects of the movie in the sense that it's essential for convincing the viewer that, despite their vastly different socioeconomic starting points, Edward and Vivian are on equal footing in terms of basic character.

Scala furthermore posits that if the two scenes leveling hero and heroine, "one grossly capitalist and mercenary, the other idealizing and ennobling," don't suffice to convince us of the feminist undertones of the film, we should also consider the possibility that it's Vivian, rather than Edward, who is the active subject of this adventure insofar as she's looking to actualize her noble character: "She is not, then, the object of the quest—the damsel in distress of the fairy tale she tells—but the questing knight."[41] In the same way that many medieval tales present the reader with a seemingly humble hero who turns out to be of noble birth, *Pretty Woman* offers the viewer a seemingly humble heroine who turns out to be of noble character. This is why, Scala concludes, "Vivian appears both as typical romance heroine *and* as something more—active, articulate, even demanding in terms of her own desire."[42]

Conspicuous consumption ("Profane, or really offensive?")

Importantly, even though Scala views Vivian as "the questing knight" of *Pretty Woman*'s fairytale, she argues—as I also have—that Vivian's transformation is not nearly as extreme as that of Edward: as I've explained, unlike Edward, Vivian doesn't need a makeover of the soul but merely a chance to actualize the fate for which she is destined. This is why Scala maintains that *Pretty Woman*'s physical makeover scenes merely denote "the always already transformed status of the heroine."[43] They merely bring Vivian's "look" in line with the inner nobility that she already possesses. This makes it doubly ironic that the Rodeo Drive shopping scene—which is explicitly about perfecting Vivian's "look"—flamboyantly foregrounds what critics have found most tactless about the movie: conspicuous consumption.

As was the case with the themes of money and gender that I analyzed above, my interpretation of *Pretty Woman*'s message about conspicuous consumption is less scathing than that of the movie's early critics. This is because the shopping scene is so utterly absurd, so completely over the top, that I can't take it seriously. Recall that outside the store that Edward has chosen for their expedition, he informs Vivian that "stores are never nice to people—they're nice to credit cards." Inside the store, he shakes hands with its manager, Mr. Hollister, thereby giving the impression that the two men are about to enter into a business deal of some kind. This detail may be one reason critics deemed the movie to be antifeminist: the two men are obviously making a pact to transform Vivian while she merely hovers meekly in the background, waiting for the action to begin. Once the formalities are over, the following dialogue ensues:

> Edward: We're gonna need a few more people helping us out. I'll tell you why. We are going to be spending an obscene amount of money in here. So we're gonna need a lot more help sucking up to us, 'cause that's what we really like. You understand?
>
> Mr. Hollister: Sir, if I may say so, you're in the right store, and the right city.

A few moments later, after Mr. Hollister has supplied Vivian with three (female) assistants and Edward with a newspaper and a cup of coffee, he deferently approaches Edward, asking, "Exactly how obscene an amount of money were you talking about? Profane, or really offensive?" "Really offensive," Edward responds. Mr. Hollister turns away, muttering, "I like him so much."

We're obviously in the realm of comedy, which is why the idea that *Pretty Woman* promotes conspicuous consumption is not entirely convincing. This isn't to say that the scene doesn't cater to the viewer's consumerist fantasy of being able to buy everything in the store. Like the "knowing wink" that, according to Susan Douglas, neutralizes the sexism of female sexual display, the comedic aspects of the scene neutralize its potentially offensive content. Yet I wouldn't say that it straightforwardly endorses consumption. Rather, it allows the viewer to participate in the fantasy of spending at the same time as it condemns those who make a habit of it; its sheer preposterousness more or less automatically makes a travesty of anyone who actually thinks that this type of consumption is the key to the good life.

For instance, Mr. Hollister's assurance that Edward is in "the right city" activates the stereotype of Los Angeles as a place where shallow people go about their superficial pursuits amidst the blaring glare of glossy surfaces. In addition, what rescues Edward's character from being ruined in the eyes of the viewer in this scene is that it implies that Edward is in reality "better than" this, that he's putting on this farcical display of consumerism because he's annoyed at how badly Vivian was treated the previous day. After all, he has already been established as a work-obsessed minimalist who leads a relatively Spartan life (doesn't sleep, do drugs, drink, or eat breakfast).

Money, in turn, counteracts the scene's sexism. Because it's Edward's money that is being spent, we're invited to forgive him for the assessing looks he directs at the clothes Vivian is considering; we're invited to overlook the fact that although he's not coercing Vivian in the same way as Scottie coerces Judy, he's guiding her choices, making sure that she'll walk out of the store meeting the specifications of what he needs his companion to look like. Viewers with any sense of clothing styles recognize that Vivian is being subtly directed toward upper-crust, conservative choices over more colorful, bolder options. Yet if we follow Scala's interpretation and accept that the shopping spree merely ensures that Vivian's appearance matches the noble character that she has always had, Edward—like Mr. Thompson earlier in the movie—becomes a fairy godmother of sorts, merely helping Vivian attain what she herself desires. Edward may not know how to turn a pumpkin into a chariot but he knows how to turn his mastercard into a magic wand that puts the gown on the girl. That he also turns out to be the one holding the glass slipper just confirms that he's good at multitasking.

The shopping sequence seduces viewers not only because it allows them to revel in a world of beautiful clothes but also because it offers the satisfaction of revenge. I mentioned earlier that one of the most beloved themes of Hollywood movies is the hero or heroine rising from the ashes. As is the case with the American dream, it's almost like the eventual victory doesn't really count unless it's preceded by seemingly insurmountable obstacles. In the original Cinderella story, one of the obstacles that Cinderella had to overcome were her evil stepsisters. In *Pretty Woman*, the snobbish sales women who refuse to serve Vivian replace the stepsisters, but revenge remains just as sweet. It's because Vivian is even lower on the socioeconomic ladder than these sales women—because she's portrayed as the true underdog of the movie—that viewers are willing to forgive Edward for scenes such as this one:

> Mr. Hollister: Mr. Lewis, sir. How's it going so far? Pretty well, I think.
> Edward: I think we need some major sucking up.
> Mr. Hollister: Very well, sir. You're not only a handsome but a powerful man. I could see the second you walked in here you were someone to reckon with.
> Edward (*pointing to Vivian*): Not me. Her.

"Not me. Her." This is the essential line, absolving Edward of the charge of being an insufferable prick.

I've stressed that we know Vivian's story before she even tells it in the sense that we understand early in the plot that such a "good" girl would never end up a hooker voluntarily. Eventually the details of her misfortune are revealed: we learn that Vivian followed a loser boyfriend to Los Angeles, got dumped, worked in a couple of fast-food restaurants, parked cars at wrestling matches, couldn't make the rent, was too ashamed to go back home, and met Kit who convinced her to become a streetwalker. We also learn that the first time she had a client, she "cried the whole time." "It's not like anybody plans this. It's not your childhood dream," she tells Edward. When Edward reassures her that she "could be so much more," she responds as follows, "People put you down enough, you start to believe it."

But we already knew all of this, didn't we? And because this is the tough hand that life unfairly dealt Vivian, we now sympathize with her efforts to transcend her lot. Her rise from a hooker to a lady becomes a metaphor for overcoming hardship—a theme that is easy to identify with. We're rooting for Vivian's Cinderella; we want her to make it because, if she does, then perhaps we can too.

Refusing the condo ("Cinde-fuckin'-rella")

Pretty Woman explicitly borrows elements of the Cinderella story at the same time as it retains a degree of ironic distance from it. In a short but crucial scene toward the end of the movie, Vivian reveals to Kit that she likes Edward so much that she's afraid of falling in love with him—indeed, may already be in love with him—and that this makes her nervous because she doesn't want to get her heart broken. When Kit—only half-jokingly—tells her that, who knows, maybe it could work out between the two of them, that maybe "you guys could, like, you know, get a house together and buy some diamonds and a horse," the following dialogue arises:

> Vivian (*slightly exasperated*): I just want to know who it works out for. You give me one example of someone we that know that it happened for.

> Kit: Name someone? You want me to name someone? You want me to, like, give you a name?
> Vivian: Yeah, I'd like a name.
> Kit (*pressing her temples, desperately trying to conjure up a name*): Oh God, the pressure of a name.... (*raising her hands in a gesture of triumph*): Cinde-fuckin'-rella.
> *Both crack up.*

The structure of this scene is comparable to that of the shopping scene I've just analyzed: in both cases, we're invited to enter into a fantasy whose utter ludicrousness we simultaneously recognize. As is the case with the theme of conspicuous consumption, the theme of romance is developed with such obvious self-mockery that the earnestness of critics such as Smith and Greenberg rings false.

I'll return to *Pretty Woman*'s ability to play both sides of the game—to have its cake and eat it too—below. But first let's take a closer look at the unfolding of its Cinderella story. The scene between Vivian and Kit I've just recounted comes after Vivian has refused Edward's offer to put her up in a condo in Los Angeles so that he can see her whenever he has to make a business trip out west. Essentially, he has proposed to make her a high-class mistress. He's proud of himself for having already arranged it all—an apartment, a car, a credit line at a variety of stores—but Vivian isn't impressed, asking, "What else? You gonna leave some money by the bed when you pass through town?" When Edward presses her to specify what she expects to happen between them, we get the longest piece of communication Vivian speaks in the movie:

> I don't know.... When I was a little girl, my mama used to lock me in the attic when I was bad, which was pretty often. And I would, I would pretend I was a princess, trapped in a tower by a wicked queen. And then, suddenly, this knight on a white horse, with these colors flying, would come charging up and draw his sword, and I would wave. And he would climb up the tower and rescue me. But never, in all the time

that I had this dream did the knight say to me, "Come on, baby. I'll put you up in a great condo."

Although I agree with Scala that, generally speaking, Vivian may be more clearly the story's questing knight than its damsel in distress, at this moment she identifies with the latter. Yet even here she holds onto her vision of how her fate should unfold, thereby remaining the questing subject who—by this late point in the narrative—has a well-defined objective. Edward initially hesitates in the face of her demand but because *Pretty Woman* is a movie that demands a happy ending, he quickly changes his mind, rides to Vivian's apartment in his white limo, and asks the famous question, "So, what happened after he climbed up the tower and rescued her?" We know her answer: "She rescues him right back."

This sequence of events showcases the negotiation between romantic fulfillment and female independence that I've proposed constitutes one of the trademarks of contemporary romantic comedies. We get our happy ending—the fairytale ending of Cinderella. But we also get an assertion of Vivian's autonomy. Arguably, this reflects a real change that has, post feminism, taken place in our romantic culture: if prior to the 1960s, many women didn't have a choice but to marry—because they quite simply had no other way of supporting themselves— women these days usually feel like they do have a choice, even if they work in low-paying jobs. *Pretty Woman* foregrounds this fact in a roundabout way, by having Vivian refuse Edward's offer even though she, in principle, has a lot to lose.

Although Vivian tells Edward that she knows that if she chose to enter into the contract of being his mistress, there would always be a guy like Phil who thought that he was entitled to sex with her, we also know that going back on the streets would expose her to similar perils. Recall that the movie portrays Hollywood Boulevard as being overrun with aggressive pimps, drug dealers, gang members, and potentially murderous johns. Against this backdrop, the fact that Vivian refuses Edward's offer of a luxury condo is a way of reminding women that they *do* have a choice, that they can survive without a man if the terms of the romantic "contract" aren't to their liking (that is, relatively equal). Critics who ridiculed *Pretty Woman*'s fairytale romance overlooked this plot element; they overlooked the fact that the movie consistently insists that if there is going to be a happy ending, it will be on Vivian's terms.

The utter cheesiness of *Pretty Woman*'s ending is also to some extent offset by the fact that the movie explicitly frames itself as a Hollywood fantasy. As I started to suggest in the context of the scene in which Kit conjures up the name of Cinderella, *Pretty Woman* self-reflexively foregrounds its reliance on fantasy. Recall the message shouted by the man in Jamaican attire at the beginning of the movie: "Welcome to Hollywood. Everybody comes to Hollywood got a dream. What's your dream?" The movie ends with the same man passing Edward and Vivian—now absorbed in their end-of-the-story kiss on Vivian's fire escape—shouting the same message: "This is Hollywood, the land of dreams. Some dreams come true, some don't. But keep on dreamin'. This is Hollywood. Always time to dream, so keep on dreamin'."

This framing marks the entire movie as a self-aware example of Hollywood's dream-making machine, of Hollywood's capacity to draw us into fantasy worlds where impossible things become possible. This machine may thwart our ability to remain critical of the messages we consume; there is no question that movies such as *Pretty Woman* influence our perception of reality, shaping our vision of how our lives should unfurl, what happiness consists of, and so on. Yet in foregrounding Hollywood's propensity for fantasy, the movie also asks us to take a degree of distance from the story we've just consumed; it asks us to recognize the distinction between fiction and reality even as we allow the fiction to linger. This is one of the many reasons I believe that women who watch it do know better—aren't duped by its romance plot any more than audiences are duped by the capacity of the seriously injured action hero to walk off the operating table so as to, minutes later, single-handedly slay the assault team that has been sent to finish him off.

Learning to shop ("I got money to spend in here")

Let me round off my analysis by focusing on aspects of *Pretty Woman* that most obviously cater to postfeminist sensibilities (and that are consequently most antithetical to either second-wave or third-wave feminism). As I've explained, postfeminist forms of neoliberal femininity rely on female sexual display and a consumerist version of the masquerade of femininity. *Pretty Woman* manages to grant viewers both: the hooker outfit Vivian wears in the first half of the movie satisfies the desire for female sexual display whereas the sumptuous wardrobe she acquires during the shopping spree—and displays throughout the rest of the movie—speaks to consumerist fantasies.

Because the movie introduces Vivian by allowing the camera to linger over the details of her scantily clad body, we know immediately that if she has any power at all—any chance of surmounting the obstacles she faces—this power is stored up in her perfect body. Her hooker outfit communicates the same idea. At the same time, the movie is feminist enough to not want to reduce Vivian to a sex object, with the consequence that it works much harder than recent romcoms to emphasize that the leading lady's sex appeal is not the main reason for the leading man's interest in her. As I'll demonstrate in greater detail below, Edward is initially bemused (rather than aroused) by Vivian's overt sexuality and is shown entering into their first sexual exchange half-reluctantly, as if he could take it or leave it. That is, the movie establishes early on that he's *not* the kind of guy who can be reduced to a stuttering idiot by the sight of a woman's bare midriff: if he were, the feminist aspects of the movie wouldn't hold.

However, this is yet another instance where the movie manages to have its cake and eat it too. Even though we're on one level being told that it's not okay to reduce Vivian to a sex object, on another level, we're invited to admire her as exactly such an object. But perhaps more importantly, the skimpy outfit Vivian wears in the first half of the movie creates the perfect backdrop for the consumerist masquerade of femininity that the second half stages: because this outfit reveals that Vivian already has the perfect body that other women work so hard to attain, it conveys that, literally, the only thing needed for her transformation, for the actualization of her "true" self, are the right clothes. As Radner remarks, "In contrast with her friend Kit, who cannot follow her into a different kind of life, Vivian's ability to wear clothes well, to 'look good,' becomes a significant sign of her worthiness and virtue."[44]

It's therefore not surprising that perhaps the main lesson Vivian learns in the course of the movie is how to shop effectively. As Radner puts it, "Vivian's education is represented by her coming to know how to shop and how to spend money."[45] Along similar lines, Chisholm notes that "the recommodification of Vivian's body from that of the prostitute who is paid for the use of her body to that of the woman who purchases items and services to redefine (and shape) her body is fundamental to the film's narrative."[46] Madonne Miner in turn asserts that Vivian "must learn how to be a good consumer."[47] More specifically, Miner maintains that one of the main messages of *Pretty Woman* is that men are supposed to produce while women are supposed to consume.

Miner's observation merits consideration in light of the argument I've made about *Pretty Woman*'s ability to subvert the dominant mantra that tells us that men and women have opposite, if complementary, characteristics and social roles. Recall that I proposed that Vivian's good driving skills and sexual assertiveness go a long way in countering our society's gender stereotypes. But I concede that when it comes to the consumerist aspects of the movie, Miner is right in proposing that the movie reinforces the traditional order of things, which insists on women's role as consumers rather than producers. "At the outset of *Pretty Woman*," Miner explains, "our main characters have gotten their economic roles confused. Edward, following a male script, should produce and perhaps, sell; Vivian, following a female script, should consume."[48] The movie then sets out to resolve this confusion.

As we've seen, Edward's problem at the beginning of the movie is that he doesn't produce anything: as Vivian observes, he doesn't make or build anything; breaking up companies to sell them piecemeal to the highest bidder is, in her opinion, "sort of like stealing cars and selling them for parts." However, by the end of the movie, Edward's transformation to a gentler capitalist has repositioned him squarely on the side of production. The movie even includes a nostalgic scene where Edward tells Phil that when he was a kid he used to love building things. In this way, the narrative suggests that because he's a man, Edward was "born" to build (isn't this why so many parents push Lego sets on their sons?). He had just somehow lost track of this fact—until Vivian reminds him of it.

I've argued that, unlike Vivian, Edward needs a makeover of the soul. This makeover is accomplished precisely by having him correct his course as a businessman so that he can start to produce. The movie explicitly aligns Edward's emotional salvation with his decision to join forces with Mr. Morse to build ships: this decision not only earns him Vivian's love but also supplies him with a supportive father figure, Mr. Morse, who declares that he's proud of Edward. As long as Edward only knows how to buy—to consume—without producing anything, he lacks both love and family; as soon as he learns to produce, both of these key ingredients of the good life are his.

In contrast, Vivian's problem at the beginning of the movie isn't just that she doesn't have enough money to consume but also that—once Edward gives her money—she doesn't know how to spend it, which—as Miner observes—violates the expected female script of being a good consumer. Conveniently, Vivian's transformation to a lady turns her from a seller (of her body) to a consumer (of things that help her enhance her body). Incidentally, the process of restoring the normative order of gender with regard to producing and consuming offers *Pretty Woman* one more way to express its ambivalence toward money: while Edward is censured for his (initial) version of laissez-faire capitalism, for wanting to destroy Mr. Morse's company, Vivian is encouraged to consume.

That Vivian initially doesn't know how to spend is foregrounded during her first, unsuccessful shopping expedition, when the sales women on Rodeo Drive instantly spot her inexpertise. In reply to her assertion that she "got money to spend in here," one of them coldly utters, "I don't think we have anything for you. You're obviously in the wrong place. Please leave." The point is developed further during Vivian's first meeting with Mr. Thompson, who tells her that she needs to dress more appropriately if she wants to stay at the hotel. In response, Vivian starts sobbing and pulls out a messy wad of dollars from her purse, saying "I have all this money now and no dress. Not that I expect you to help me, but I have all of this, Ok? I have to buy a dress for dinner tonight, and nobody will help me."

Everything from Vivian's pathetic bundle of money to her inability to spend it suggests that she hasn't mastered the all-important feminine art of shopping. Nor has she mastered the art of creating a feminine identity through frequent wardrobe changes (isn't it to teach their daughters this lesson that parents push Barbie dolls on them?). In obvious breach of feminine protocol, she wears the same outfit from Hollywood Boulevard to Rodeo Drive and—even worse!—two days in a row. Mr. Thompson takes pity on her, picks up his magic wand (the telephone), and conjures into existence an obliging sales woman named Bridget, who—because, unlike Vivian, she has mastered the details of consumer savvy—instantly knows that Vivian is a size six. Vivian's amazement at this only highlights her inexperience further, for women are usually not surprised when sales personnel guess their size correctly. After all, we know that, as Bridget explains, it's their job.

The second Rodeo Drive shopping expedition demonstrates Vivian's progress from a woman who simply doesn't know how to spend money to one who both excels and takes pleasure in doing so. However, Miner is right to propose that "the purchase that crowns Vivian's career as buyer is that of a husband."[49] At the beginning of the movie, Vivian doesn't understand her own worth, thinking that a hundred dollars an hour is an extravagant sum to pay for her services, even for a man as wealthy as Edward. When he asks her to stay the whole week, she's still asking for less than he's willing to pay: he specifies that he would have paid four thousand instead of the three she agrees to. However, by the end of the week, things have changed drastically. Edward is now offering a great deal more: a condo, a car, and a generous shopping allowance. But Vivian has learned to drive a hard bargain, stating, "You made me a really nice offer. And a few months ago, no problem, but now everything is different and you changed that and you can't change back. I want more."

Vivian is no longer willing to undersell herself. She wants the whole fairytale: the prince and the happily ever after. Even when Edward appeals to her affection, begging her to stay one more night, not because he's paying her to but because she wants to, she holds her ground and refuses. Miner observes:

> According to the "separate spheres" logic of the film, Vivian's refusal is right; she cannot afford affection (whereas Edward can no longer afford to be without it) if it costs her a wedding ring. Capitulation means she purchases an inferior product—a night with Edward rather than life as his wife; all she has learned about entrepreneurship mandates that she hold out for the latter.[50]

Miner's final assessment of Vivian's choice to marry Edward (though Edward never proposes on screen, the assumption is that he will) is the same as that of Greenberg: Vivian merely swaps one form of prostitution for another. Noting that as a prostitute, Vivian can still say when, who, and how much, but that as Edward's wife, she gives up that right, Miner argues that Vivian buys herself a marriage contract "at the cost of body and soul."[51] In this manner, Miner, like Greenberg, suggests—as some second-wave feminists also did—that marriage is merely a socially glorified form of prostitution, a contract through which women offer sexual services in return for their husband's money. Fortunately, things have changed for the better: it would be difficult to make this argument about many modern marriages. But in the world of *Pretty Woman*, the logic admittedly still holds to some extent.

Jane Caputi pushes this line of reasoning to its limit through a comparison between *Pretty Woman* and another Julia Roberts movie, *Sleeping with the Enemy* (1991). Caputi argues that *Pretty Woman* is a prelude of sorts to *Sleeping with the Enemy*, which is a movie about a battered woman, Laura (Roberts) who is desperate to escape her jealous, controlling, and violent husband, Martin. Martin treats Laura as a prized possession, threatening to kill her if she ever leaves him. He's obsessively preoccupied with Laura's dress, appearance, and mannerisms, attempting to monitor every aspect of her being. Caputi proposes that *Pretty Woman*'s Edward can be read as a premarriage edition of Martin: like Martin, he controls Vivian's dress, appearance, and mannerisms, closely monitoring her behavior. And when he finally falls in love with her, it's because he realizes that she's comparable to the necklace he had borrowed for the night at the opera—that she is, in effect, a prized possession.

In Caputi's view, Edward regards women as objects to make use of. Asserting that "nearly all texts on wife battery warn women against the whirlwind romance and bonding to a man whom one knows only slightly," Caputi portrays Edward as a precursor to Martin because he possesses characteristics that predispose him to be abusive.[52] Among these Caputi lists his highly organized, controlled approach to the world; his history of family trauma; his anger toward his father; his previous relationship trouble; and his jealousy when he catches Vivian talking to David, Mr. Morse's grandson, at the polo match.

All of this leads Caputi to declare that "Edward and Vivian's relationship is one based purely in male power and female submission. . . . She is his sexual servant."[53] *Sleeping with the Enemy*, in turn, is what happens when "the princess wakes up."[54] Incidentally, Martin calls Laura a princess.

As should be clear by now, I'm not fond of this type of "realistic" reading, backed up by statistics about battered women and psychological portraits of abusive men. Indeed, if I believed that every organized guy who has trouble sustaining a relationship is predestined to become a wife-beater, I'd have to stop talking to most of my male friends. Nor am I convinced that Edward and Vivian's relationship is purely a matter of male power and female submission. As I've illustrated, there are plenty of major plot elements in the movie that indicate the opposite. This is why it feels like an overextension of social realism to argue, as Caputi does, that it won't be long before Edward starts abusing Vivian: "How long will it be before Edward again treats Vivian 'like a prostitute,' perhaps accusing her of thwarting his business deals, impugning her as a whore, beating her, and raping her? Like Martin, probably he'll wait until after the honeymoon."[55]

Vivian as fetish ("Something's missing")

This type of speculation beyond the film's frame seems pointless: Edward and Vivian are not real people, so it's futile to try to guess how they'll behave beyond the narrative. A better way to use feminist insights to analyze *Pretty Woman* might be to employ some of the tools of psychoanalytic film theory that I introduced in the previous chapter. Consider, for instance, the role that both voyeurism and fetishism play in the movie.

For starters, Vivian is consistently depicted as the object of Edward's voyeuristic (sometimes curious, other times appraising) gaze. Edward observes Vivian sleeping, eating, bathing, singing, and watching the opera. When he suspects her of having brought drugs into his hotel room, he insists she show him what she's holding (it turns out that this is a box of dental floss). This is the one scene in the movie that might support Caputi's domestic battery hypothesis, for it exhibits the kind of male aggression that psychoanalytic theorists have associated with voyeurism.

Edward also obviously assesses Vivian's appearance throughout the movie, not just when they go shopping but also before each major outing: the dinner with Mr. Morse, the polo match, and the evening at the opera. Before the opera, Edward literally walks half way around Vivian, who is wearing her body-hugging red gown, to appraise her figure, finally announcing, "Something's missing"? When she replies that "nothing else is gonna fit into this dress," he pulls out a jewelry box that contains the aforementioned ruby necklace worth a quarter of a million dollars. One doesn't need to go as far as Freud did when he, in his famous interpretation of the case of Dora, compared female genitalia to a jewelry box to propose that this is a scene of fetishism: an attempt to make sure that the woman is not missing anything essential.[56] The necklace serves as a fetish object that "completes" the woman at the same time as it completes her outfit.

In this way, *Pretty Woman* fairly overtly suggests that Vivian can only complete—rescue—Edward if she's herself complete. Recall that, from a Lacanian perspective, it's possible to read the heteropatriarchal fantasy that men and women are capable of completing each other as an attempt to cope with the fundamental (ontological) lack that haunts human subjectivity. Recall also that the major glitch in this fantasy is that woman is, culturally speaking, deemed to be so *drastically* lacking that only an elaborate structure of fetishism can keep the male fantasy of being completed by her intact. As we learned, fetishism covers over the woman's lack (castration) so that the man doesn't need to face the threat posed by her, including the possibility that she might take revenge on his dominance by castrating him, as Lorena

Bobbitt did in 1993 when she took a searing knife to her abusive husband's penis.

In the context of *Pretty Woman*'s mutual rescue theme, all of this implies that Vivian can't be found lacking: if Edward's ability to rescue Vivian depends on his wealth, Vivian's ability to rescue Edward—who, as I've argued, is depicted as being emotionally lost—depends on her capacity to incarnate the perfect woman, that is, on her capacity to meet the requirements of his fantasy. Edward's assessment of Vivian in the necklace scene—"something's missing"—arguably represents a literal rendering of the structure of fetishism: it's as if Edward is telling Vivian that, without the necklace, she's indeed lacking in ways that are unacceptable, that will keep him from falling in love with her. Once the necklace has been placed on Vivian, she's ready to fill the void of Edward's barren life. It's then fitting that it's when Mr. Thompson admires the necklace toward the end of the movie that Edward realizes that he's in love with Vivian. If love is impossible without the necklace, then it may not be strange that it's the necklace, rather than the woman herself, that elicits the feeling of love.

Jane O'Sullivan proposes that *Pretty Woman* highlights the anxiety that underlies the male lover's fetishistic efforts to attain and subsequently control the perfect woman. Relying on Freud's insight that fetishization allows the fetishist to both acknowledge the female body as lacking and to disavow this lack in order to experience pleasure, O'Sullivan calls attention to the suspension of belief that enables Edward to fall in love with the fantasy he has created. More specifically, O'Sullivan remarks that Edward falls for Vivian despite his "incontrovertible knowledge of her status as a hooker."[57] She adds that "this kind of self-deception is not unlike the suspension of disbelief that may be required of viewers if the otherwise unlikely romantic resolution of the film is to be in any way convincing."[58]

O'Sullivan hence explains viewers' willingness to enter into the fantasy world of movies like *Pretty Woman* by drawing a parallel between the male fetishist's relationship to the female body and the audience's relationship to the narrative they're watching. It's worth noting the manner in which narcissism enters into this comparison: the male fetishist falls in love with his own idealized creation whereas the audience gets sutured into idealized alter egos on the screen. Narcissism, in this sense, may be intrinsically fetishistic, dependent on fetishization's capacity to conjure away lack (imperfection). To put the matter more concretely, we know that the perfection of our alter egos is fantasmatic—and we may even know exactly when Shelley Michelle's body is substituted for the body of Julia Roberts—but we want to believe in the flawlessness of what we see anyway.

This reading of fetishism brings us back to Kaja Silverman's conceptualization of suture as one manifestation of our desire for regained wholeness. I suspect that this desire, in part at least, explains the popularity of movies that tell stories of defeat and eventual (hard-won) victory: perhaps the story of rising from rags to riches, from lack to plenitude, on some level speaks to the fantasy of being wounded and then made whole again. From this viewpoint, the American dream of overcoming all obstacles may not be merely a capitalist fantasy but also a foundational fantasy of subjectivity. But consumer capitalism certainly helps sustain it, which is why romcoms like *Pretty Woman* enact a deeply commercial version of the masquerade of femininity, implying that a woman can be made whole by a trip to an expensive store. In this sense, labels such as Louis Vuitton, Chanel, Diamonds on Rodeo, and Gucci—labels that *Pretty Woman* foregrounds—are not merely names but connote the promise of self-fulfillment and self-completion.

According to O'Sullivan, the price of this commercial version of femininity can sometimes be even higher than what the tags on the luxury items connected to such labels indicate. Comparing *Vertigo* and *Pretty Woman*, O'Sullivan argues that the attempts of Scottie and Edward to fashion a perfect female companion effectively tame, restrict, and devitalize their objects of desire. We've seen that this theme is more pronounced in *Vertigo*, where Scottie's demands upon Judy rob her of personality. *Pretty Woman*, in contrast, counters the chilling effects of fetishization by ensuring that Vivian's vivacious personality persists underneath her costumes; she never seamlessly disappears into her masquerade. But it's still true that the more Vivian approximates Edward's ideal, the more subdued her demeanor becomes.

O'Sullivan states:

> As Vivian and Judy squeeze themselves into little black cocktail dresses and appropriate manners and mannerisms for their respective roles as the "perfect dinner date" for the men who have fashioned them, each can be seen as fitting into a mold of femininity the outer limits of which function as a kind of restraint that only allows for a lesser version of herself.[59]

In other words, when Vivian fully steps into the masquerade of femininity, she, like Judy, sacrifices some of her liveliness and spontaneity. The more Vivian is evaluated by Edward, the more careful—the more constrained in her behavior—she becomes. In this sense, O'Sullivan is correct that "there is something of the lifeless mannequin about Vivian when she is most convincingly presenting a masquerade of femininity."[60]

The male gaze ("You're stunning")

Because of *Pretty Woman*'s emphasis on the commercial construction of femininity, it's not surprising that one of its most notable characteristics is that it activates the male gaze primarily through consumption. When Edward first meets Vivian, he is—significantly—not looking at her but at the gears of his car. In addition, as I mentioned earlier, his response to her hooker version of femininity is lukewarm at best. We understand that he's not the kind of guy who would normally cruise Hollywood Boulevard to pick up prostitutes. But we're also led to intuit that because he comes from the refined world of the extremely rich, hooker-Vivian's vulgar version of blatantly sexual femininity doesn't hold much appeal for him.

I don't mean to imply that Edward—or the movie at large—condemns active female sexuality. Quite the contrary, I stand behind my earlier suggestion that *Pretty Woman* offers a refreshingly nonjudgmental portrayal of female sexual assertiveness. At the same time, the movie's commercial ethos dictates that Vivian must learn to stage the masquerade of femininity in a way that corresponds to Edward's upper-class predilections: according to *Pretty Woman*'s vision of the good life, you're not going to land a husband when a safety pin is holding up the zipper of your boot; romance is, rather, the result of spending money and of looking feminine in the right—elegant—way.

Even when Edward escorts Vivian into his hotel suite after the driving scene, he initially has no sexual interest in her, looking through his mail instead. This confuses her because she assumes that he has invited her in for sex, and the humor of the scene arises from her efforts to hurry the process along and his efforts to slow it down: he orders champagne and strawberries; she pulls out her colorful "buffet" of condoms in the hope that this will move him in the right direction. When it doesn't—when he tells her that he would prefer to chat—she responds, "I appreciate this whole seduction scene you've got going, but let me give you a tip. I'm a sure thing. I'm on an hourly rate. Can we just move it along?"

This is when Edward offers to pay Vivian for the whole night so that she'll stop worrying about how much time it's taking. In reply, Vivian says, "Are you sure you want me to stay for the entire night? I mean, I could just pop you good and be on my way." Can you see why I don't think that this is your average romantic comedy? More to the point, even when Edward finally acquiesces to getting a blowjob, we get the sense that he does so mostly because he has nothing better to do. Desire plays no part. In fact, when she approaches him—on her knees—he pulls out a lock of her blonde hair and looks at it with a mixture of curiosity and disdain. Although he doesn't at this point realize that she's wearing a wig, there is something about her hair that isn't quite right: it's too fake, too tasteless. So, yes, he deigns to receive her services, but there is no sign of passion; it's more like he doesn't care enough to refuse.

All of this changes the following night, when Edward meets Vivian at the hotel bar to take her to the dinner with Mr. Morse. At this point, she's wearing the chic cocktail dress that Mr. Thompson has helped her procure, her red hair is elegantly styled, and her makeup is understated. He gives her a long and approving look: this is the first time within the film's narrative that the male gaze is activated in earnest. For the spectators this gaze has been active since the opening sequence lingering on Vivian's body but this is the first time that Edward looks at Vivian with genuine interest. The succinct exchange that follows confirms that she finally has his attention:

Vivian: You're late.
Edward: You're stunning.
Vivian: You're forgiven.

Simple but effective. We now know—as does Vivian—what kind of woman will rouse Edward's desire: the polished and graceful kind. And we also know that Vivian welcomes the male gaze as a compliment.

The theme of commercially generated femininity—that is, neoliberal femininity—eliciting male desire continues throughout the movie. At every step of Vivian's physical transformation, we witness Edward assessing her approvingly, as in the scene with the red gown and ruby necklace. The premise of their contract—that she has to convincingly fit the part of Edward's companion—creates a space for scenes where Edward is allowed to explicitly appraise Vivian's attractiveness without this offending her or the female spectator. In addition, we get to witness the gazes of numerous other men looking at her appreciatively, as is the case when she exits the Rodeo Drive boutique after her triumphant shopping spree and when she walks across the hotel lobby in her red gown.

The latter is the scene that most explicitly foregrounds the male gaze, for it begins by one of the (male) hotel employees alerting his two coworkers, both male, to the fact that an attractive woman has just entered the lobby. This is a common enough occurrence, not just in movies but also in real life. *Pretty Woman* presents it as a flattering thing, which is not necessarily how it feels when one is passing a bunch of construction workers on the street. Because this part of *Pretty Woman* is set in the world of high society, where people are supposed to behave courteously (even if they sometimes don't), it manages to neutralize the discomfort that the male gaze can cause women in the real world, making it seem like being evaluated by unknown men is a privilege. The admiring gaze here is depicted as harmless, divorced from the sting of objectification and denigration that often accompanies it in the real world; it's presented as what every woman should want, given that—recall—every woman's desire (supposedly) is to be desired.

The lobby scene, additionally, desexualizes the gaze by having one of the female employees nudge another woman to pay attention so that both of them get to admire Vivian as she makes her way through the lobby. In this way, the movie deftly defuses the misogynistic connotations of the male gaze by signaling that the men in the lobby aren't doing anything different from what the female employees are doing: they're all just innocently admiring beauty. Finally, even though Vivian is the object of the spectator's gaze from the get-go, the fact that this spectator is presumed to be female and straight—even if this isn't always the case in reality—means that her gaze is expected to be one of identification rather than of sexual desire: female spectators aren't expected to want to have sex with Vivian; they're expected to want to look like her so that they can elicit male desire.

It's then all the more significant that male desire is largely absent in the opening scenes of the movie—the scenes where Vivian is showing a lot of skin. In these scenes, she's assessed by men only as being inappropriately dressed (so not as an object of desire). The male gaze—and the desire that it's supposed to connote—only gets mobilized when crude sexuality is replaced by the sophistication of commercial femininity. Again, this may in part be due to *Pretty Woman*'s complicated allegiance to second-wave feminism: the fact that it doesn't want to present its heroine as a sex object. At the same time, it's how the movie communicates to straight female viewers that female desirability is connected to spending money. If there is a physical lack—castration—to be covered over through a fetishistic enactment of the masquerade of femininity, there is also another kind of lack that needs to be concealed: the dearth of resources. The neoliberal fetish object must exude affluence above all things. No wonder that Mr. Thompson beams proudly when Vivian emerges from her second Rodeo Drive expedition overpowered by shopping bags.

Not coincidentally, after *Pretty Woman*'s release, designers reproduced many of Vivian's outfits, making them—including the famous Pretty Woman boots—available to ordinary women. (As a side note, it's interesting to think about why the item of clothing, the boots, that doesn't elicit male desire within the movie narrative was what most appealed to female consumers outside the movie.) By now, this practice of producing replicas of consumer items first introduced in movies and television shows has become a common feature of media culture. Actresses such as Sarah Jessica Parker have made their name less on their acting skills than on their skill as fashion trendmakers. Conversely, designers actively seek to place their products in movies and television shows, which is why these often include ridiculously overt references to specific cars, watches, and other luxury items. When every cast member in a television show is driving a Mercedes, we know that it's not just because they all work at the same FBI office.

In romantic comedies, Harry Winston jewelry has been one of the most aggressively marketed products so that spectators who routinely watch them have come to expect the "Harry Winston moment" when the female lead for whatever convoluted reason gets to wear one of the designer's necklaces or bracelets, or—if she about to live happily ever after—one of his engagement rings. "Harry Winston," in the romcom universe, has come to be synonymous with "truly making it" as a woman, as a subject of neoliberal femininity. Tiffany's holds a—not so shabby—second place.

Humanizing the heroine ("Stop fidgeting and smile")

In such a context—a context that links the masquerade of femininity to what many would see as crass commercialism—it's important to find ways to humanize the heroine. The masquerade of femininity always raises the specter of artificiality, and when it's connected to consumerism, it risks robbing the romcom heroine of the likeability that is required of her. In addition, as L'Oreal's famous ad implies, being too beautiful might cause one to be hated. The emphasis on female solidarity that many romantic comedies display is one way to counter this: the loyal female friends of a romcom heroine never resent her for her attractiveness. Another common strategy is to render the heroine slightly flawed, frequently through a detail that is repeated throughout the film.

For instance, in *Miss Congeniality*, Gracie's clumsiness and brassiness keep her pleasantly human even when she sports glamorous clothes that make her so beautiful that the average female viewer might begin to hate her a little. When Gracie emerges from her labor-intensive makeover in an airplane hangar—where she has been plucked, waxed, styled, makeuped, and dressed by an army of professionals—all eyes, including the stunned eyes of her love-interest-to-be Eric, are on her. Dressed in a figure-hugging blue miniskirt and her long locks flowing, she utters, "I'm haven't eaten in two days, I haven't slept, I'm wearing high heels and hair gel, don't mess with me," after which she stumbles and falls to the ground, to the appreciative amusement of everyone.

This combination of clumsiness and brassiness is repeated throughout *Miss Congeniality*, and it makes Gracie one of the most likable female leads in recent movie history. *Legally Blonde*'s commercially generated femininity is likewise mitigated by a scene of utter embarrassment: Elle (Reese Witherspoon) shows up at a Harvard Law School party wearing a pink bunny outfit because a mean girl has tricked her into thinking that she was going to a costume party. Similar details could be lifted from most romantic comedies, and their purpose is always to keep the female protagonist likable even when she's impossibly attractive.

Pretty Woman resorts to the same strategy, in part by including a number of scenes of minor humiliation, such as when Vivian doesn't know which fork to use, when she flings a snail across the Voltaire, when she doesn't realize that she's supposed to tip the waiter who delivers room service, and when Edward catches her singing off-key in his bathtub. In *Pretty Woman*, this strategy is also applied to Edward: he's kept likable by his little flaws. His otherwise confident—almost arrogant—demeanor is humanized not just by his inability to drive a stick shift but also by his fear of heights and—to complete the imagery of phallic failure—his stumbling attempts to make his key card open the door of his penthouse suite.

However, what is particularly interesting is that *Pretty Woman* accomplishes Vivian's humanization most effectively by revealing her slight discomfort with the very commercial rendition of the masquerade of femininity that the movie otherwise valorizes: she can't stop fidgeting. This is the detail that Roger Ebert is commenting on when he states that the movie gives Vivian's "character an irrepressibly bouncy sense of humor and then lets her spend the movie trying to repress it." And it's the aspect of the movie that O'Sullivan draws attention to when she argues that Vivian's makeover drains her of her vitality.

Although O'Sullivan is right, Ebert captures something she overlooks, namely that *Pretty Woman* does this on purpose.

Like *Vertigo*, it's on some level a commentary on the discomfort entailed in the construction of normative femininity. Or more specifically, it once again manages to have things both ways: we get to appreciate Vivian's transformation at the same time as we're subtly made aware of its problematic undertones.

Vivian is shown to be entirely comfortable in her hooker outfit—not in the least bit embarrassed by it or apologetic for it, even in Edward's posh hotel. But the minute she starts to dress "up," her body language changes from confident to slightly fidgety. Edward's "stop fidgeting" becomes a repeating refrain in the movie, for he utters it when they enter the Voltaire, when they're about to enter the polo match—"don't fidget and smile"—and when they cross the hotel lobby on their way to the opera: "When you're not fidgeting, you look very beautiful."

All this ordering is potentially annoying to female spectators, and if it doesn't become so, this is because Vivian's fidgeting serves two important functions: (1) it acknowledges the anxiety caused by the masquerade of femininity, thereby earning the sympathies of female spectators who may be familiar with this anxiety, and (2) it cracks the façade of Vivian's masquerade of high-class femininity just enough to keep her likable even when she embodies the feminine ideal to a degree that real women can't easily emulate.

Revealing that you're not perfect at the masquerade of femininity—revealing that the masquerade makes you struggle a bit and that you even somewhat resent its demands—is one of the fastest ways to humanize a female lead. This is because many female spectators aren't perfect at it, struggle with it, and somewhat resent its demands. Women in our society engage with the masquerade of femininity to varying degrees, but those who use it to build their identities (presumably) rarely feel like they have mastered it. There may be moments of mastery, as when you first enter a party. But then your mascara starts to smudge, your armpits start to sweat, your foundation starts to melt, and your lipstick finds its way to the rim of your wine glass.

In real life, the masquerade of femininity is virtually impossible to sustain over long stretches of time, which is why it's nice to watch screen icons also struggle with it. Julia Roberts struggles with it quite convincingly in *Pretty Woman*, which is why I've always thought that she should have won an Oscar for this movie rather than for her 2000 *Erin Brockovich* (a more "serious" movie but arguably not Roberts's best performance). It's easy to assume that if you happen to be attractive, playing a romcom heroine is a no-brainer. But I would say that it takes considerable acting skills to successfully portray the tensions that I've flagged as being central to the romcom universe: between femininity and feminism, romance and independence, and the masquerade of femininity and the flawed humanity that this masquerade seeks to conceal.

I've always thought that Julia Roberts's capacity to look amazing at the same time as she looks slightly uncomfortable showcases her talent as an actress—something that is important to stress for the simple reason that romcom leads are frequently ridiculed for their bad acting in the same way that the genre, overall, is ridiculed for being shallow. The fact is that actresses such as Sandra Bullock, Cameron Diaz, Anne Hathaway, Anna Kendrick, Emma Stone, and Reese Witherspoon have been so popular with Hollywood directors and female audiences alike not only because they're beautiful but also because they're able to combine looking great with looking clumsy, awkward, anxious, or even humiliated; they're good at remaining ordinary even when the movie narrative presents them as being out of the ordinary. Ebert is right to claim that actresses who manage this "can have whatever they want in Hollywood."

Conclusion

I've attempted to illustrate that romantic comedies are difficult to categorize as either regressive or progressive, that they often contain a hefty serving of feminist elements even as they celebrate traditional romance, hyperfemininity, shopping, and other themes that can be hard to reconcile with feminism. One could even argue that the capacity of romantic comedies to consistently have it both ways explains why they're so successful. In other words, if so many women like these movies, it's not just because they've been taught to take pleasure in their own objectification or because heteropatriarchy has brainwashed them to accept the fantasy of the happily ever after; it's also because many romcoms contain genuinely liberatory, empowering messages. Although there is almost always a way to argue, like many of the early critics of *Pretty Woman* did, that romantic comedies offer a backhanded version of misogyny, my sense is that if things were this simple, female viewers wouldn't be so captivated.

I've demonstrated that one reason *Pretty Woman* "works" on many levels is that it skillfully negotiates seemingly contrasting attitudes: it revels in conspicuous consumption yet also subtly frowns upon it; it relies on a fairytale romance yet gently mocks the parameters of the Cinderella story; it objectifies the female body yet presents its male lead as being largely uninterested in an overtly sexualized version of femininity; it indulges in the masquerade of femininity yet discloses the discomfort that this masquerade causes. At every step of the way, it invites us to enter into its fantasy at the same time as it pushes this fantasy so far that it's hard to take it entirely seriously. Moreover, it dexterously navigates the desire for a combination of female independence and girly femininity that characterizes the postfeminist world: in giving us a sexually assertive, outspoken, and autonomous heroine who also happens to look stunning in an opera gown, it covers a lot of bases. As I said in the Introduction, this doesn't make it the best movie ever made. But it's also definitely not as stupid as many of its critics have made it out to be.

It's true that movies like *Pretty Woman* shape our understanding of the good life. It's undoubtedly true that they're a major instrument in the biopolitical conditioning of American women. It may even be true that the fantasy world of romcoms—replete with handsome men who also turn out to be caring, sensitive, and generous—indoctrinates women to have overly idealistic expectations of men. But I've sought to illustrate that this aspect of romcoms can be viewed as an attempt to build a utopia of gender relations that reaches beyond the battle of the sexes; it can be seen as an attempt to envision a world where men and women share much more with each other than our culture, so attached to stereotypes about "natural" gender differences, is willing to admit. Among other things, the romcom world is one where men are willing to talk about their emotions and where women initiate sex. I'm not sure that this world is antifeminist.

In Chapter 1, we saw that Susan Douglas believes that young women miss feminism without realizing it, that in the absence of feminism they have no way to express their rage about our society's ideals of femininity. This may well be true. I would merely add that women might miss feminism in another sense as well: as an intellectual and political movement that strove to deconstruct the divide between men and women so as to open up more capacious ways of inhabiting the world for everyone. An important part of this (third-wave) feminist enterprise was to neutralize the power struggle between men and women by illustrating that all of us are victims of heteropatriarchy's investment in rigid gender roles. This is why third-wave feminism saw progressive men as potential allies.

CONCLUSION

In our postfeminist world, this third-wave feminist vision is losing ground to factions of our society, such as self-help authors, popular scientists, and online bloggers, that are keen to make a profit from the endless recycling of gender stereotypes, including the idea that to make romance work, we need to learn to dissect the mystifying, gender-specific motivations of the "opposite" sex. Even if the norms of gender are loosening up among some segments of the population (genderqueers, urban hipsters, film studies majors, and so on), other segments remain persuaded by long-standing stereotypes. Within this cultural terrain, romantic comedies are among the few mainstream venues that fairly dependably side with the third-wave feminist vision. This doesn't make them feminist per se. Nor are their feminist components necessarily very sophisticated. But given the dearth of alternatives, I would propose that many of the women who consume them are not so much turning away from feminism as they're trying to keep some part of it alive.

Sara Ahmed maintains that giving up dominant happiness scripts isn't a matter of becoming unhappy but rather of reimagining the meaning of happiness, of making room for a different kind of life.[1] At first glance, romcoms are a bad candidate for such a reinvention of the world in the sense that they tend to promote the happiness scripts of neoliberal capitalism, fulfillment via consumerism, and heteronormative romance. But if we switch to a lens that focuses on gender relations specifically, we find a different picture: we find that romcoms offer a surprisingly promising terrain for revamping our understanding of the good life because, as I've argued, they tend to break our society's gender norms more consistently than they uphold them. Indeed, there is a degree of irony to the fact that it's romantic comedies—the Hollywood genre that has historically been the most disparaged for being sentimental drivel directed at stupid female audiences—that remain more overtly feminist than much of the rest of Hollywood.

Romantic comedies remind women that the current order of things is not the only possible order. Yes, they are unrealistic.

But sometimes it's hard to say what's realistic. Did women in the 1950s know that in a matter of decades, women's lives would change beyond recognition? My mother once told me that she envies my generation of women not just because we get to do a lot of things that she didn't get to do but also because we—at least those of us who are able to dodge the ideology of gender stereotyping—get to interact with men who for the most part view us as equal creatures. Similarly, I sometimes envy my twenty-year-old female students because I can tell that many of the twenty-year-old guys they're hanging out with are pretty cool about gender, even cooler than most men my age. This demonstrates that something that might have seemed impossible just a couple of generations ago has become possible.

In large part, cultural improvements in gender relations are due to the victories of feminism. But in some part, they're also due to the fact that mass entertainment has bombarded us with images of cool guys at least since the early 1990s, the era of *Pretty Woman*. Today's men may get much of their education about gender from online pornography. But they get at least some of it from movies and television shows—if not romcoms specifically, then at least from television shows that resemble romcoms. This is an instance in which our much-maligned lowbrow entertainment system is arguably doing some good.

Finally, I would propose that romantic comedies speak to a fantasy that is in danger of being lost in today's overly pragmatic society, namely the fantasy of the kind of sublime love that transcends the parameters of everyday life. The French philosopher Alain Badiou talks about love as a transformative "event" that makes it impossible for the person who has fallen in love to continue living in the same way as he or she always has. Love as an event of this kind brings about a drastic reconfiguration of the lover's entire universe, demanding, among other things, that this universe accommodate the all-important presence of the beloved.[2]

This presence of the beloved may sometimes be inconvenient, for those we love don't always act in the way that we would like them to act, but the kind of love Badiou is talking about doesn't buckle under the annoyances of relationality. It also doesn't yield in the face of social conventions, such as expectations about the type of person one is supposed to love. Most importantly, such love rises above the banalities of the kind of emotional manipulation that frequently characterizes modern relationships, striking the lover with the force of a nonnegotiable (and therefore nonmanipulable) truth.

This notion of love is antithetical to the vision of love as a labor-intensive endeavor that I criticized in Chapter 1. And it also counters the idea of love as a calculated game that has taken over our self-help industry. Both of these dominant conceptions are doing well in our society because of this society's neoliberal emphasis on levelheaded efficiency; they offer an image of romance that makes sense to people who are used to thinking that they should be able to control everything from their jobs to their bodies to their love lives. This is a romantic culture that presents being derailed by passion as a risk that needs to be counteracted, which is precisely why it encourages us to approach our relationships with the strategic acumen of chess players.

Romantic comedies such as *Pretty Woman* are among the few cultural forces that are still putting up a resistance to this new status quo of love, that are still insisting that love should be more ardent than the overly sensible dating scene of today's society—a scene where people have often been matched by computer-generated sheets of compatibility and where they're doing everything in their power to anticipate the move that the other party is going to make next; if contemporary couples often approach dating with the same rational attitude as they apply to their income taxes, romcoms celebrate love's more irrational side. It's perhaps because we aren't yet entirely ready to discard this side that we're willing to accept their (admittedly outlandish) fictions.

NOTES

Introduction

1 Helen Warner, "'A New Feminist Revolution in Hollywood Comedy'?: Postfeminist Discourses and the Critical Reception of *Bridesmaids*," in *Postfeminism and Contemporary Hollywood Cinema*, ed. Joel Gwynne and Nadine Muller (London: Palgrave Macmillan, 2013), 266.

2 This statement can be found on the DVD cover of *Bridesmaids*.

3 Warner, "'A New Feminist Revolution in Hollywood Comedy,'" 288.

4 Ibid., 229.

5 Ibid., 231.

6 Diane Negra, "Structural Integrity, Historical Reversion, and the Post-9/11 Chick Flick," *Feminist Media Studies* 8, no. 1 (2008): 51.

7 Tamar Jeffers McDonald, *Romantic Comedy: Boy Meets Girl Meets Genre* (London: Wallflower, 2002), 7.

8 Warner, "'A New Feminist Revolution in Hollywood Comedy,'" 222.

9 Hilary Radner, *Neo-Feminist Cinema: Girly Films, Chick Flicks, and Consumer Culture* (New York: Routledge, 2011), 41.

10 Ibid., 28.

11 Ibid., 40.

12 The screwball comedies of the 1930s and the 1940s are arguably more straightforwardly feminist than many contemporary romantic comedies. However, even they often end in a manner that "tames" the female lead, usually through a romantic

resolution. This is the case, for instance, in *Bringing Up Baby* and *His Girl Friday*.

13 Being a "cis-man" or "cis-woman" means that your gender presentation falls within our culture's heteronormative understanding of gender. For instance, a traditionally "masculine" gay man who "reads" as straight is a "cis-man" even though he's gay. Being "genderqueer," in turn, means that your gender presentation falls outside of our culture's heteronormative definition of gender. A straight woman who comes across as "masculine" is "genderqueer" even though she's straight.

14 For a critique of the wave model of feminist history, see Leela Fernandes, *Transnational Feminism in the United States: Knowledge, Ethics, Power* (New York: NYU Press, 2013).

15 Susan Douglas, *The Rise of Enlightened Sexism: How Pop Culture Took Us from Girl Power to Girls Gone Wild* (New York: St. Martin's Griffin, 2010).

16 See Mari Ruti, *The Ethics of Opting Out: Queer Theory's Defiant Subjects* (New York: Columbia University Press, forthcoming).

Chapter 1

1 Molly Haskell, *From Reverence to Rape: The Treatment of Women in the Movies* (Chicago: University of Chicago Press, 1974), 1–2.

2 See Sigmund Freud, *Five Lectures on Psychoanalysis*, trans. James Strachey (New York: Norton, 1961).

3 For a brilliant analysis of the ideology of gender complementarity, see Hilary Neroni, *The Violent Woman: Femininity, Narrative, and Violence in Contemporary American Cinema* (Albany, NY: SUNY Press, 2005).

4 See Christopher Ryan and Cacilda Jethá, *Sex at Dawn: The Prehistoric Origins of Modern Sexuality* (New York: Harper, 2011).

5 The details of the female Oedipus complex are beyond the parameters of this book. Suffice it to say that, like the male

Oedipus complex, the female Oedipus complex aims at normative (gender-bifurcated) heterosexuality.

6   Ernest Jones, *Sigmund Freud: Life and Work* (London: Hogarth Press, 1953), 421.

7   Simone de Beauvoir, *The Second Sex*, trans. Constance Borde and Sheila Malovany-Chevallier (New York: Alfred A. Knopf, 2010), 283. This text was originally published in 1949.

8   See Jacques Lacan, "The Instance of the Letter in the Unconscious, or Reason Since Freud," in *Écrits: The First Complete Edition in English*, trans. Bruce Fink (New York: Norton, 2007), 412–44.

9   See Jacques Lacan, "The Signification of the Phallus," in *Écrits: The First Complete Edition in English*, trans. Bruce Fink (New York: Norton, 2007), 575–84.

10 Kaja Silverman, *The Subject of Semiotics* (Oxford: Oxford University Press, 1983), 212.

11 Ibid., 236.

12 Ibid., 221.

13 Teresa de Lauretis, "Oedipus Interruptus," in *Feminist Film Theory: A Reader*, ed. Sue Thornham (New York: New York University Press, 1999), 85. The selection is from de Lauretis's book *Alice Doesn't: Feminism, Semiotics, Cinema* (Bloomington: Indiana University Press, 1984).

14 Ibid., 93.

15 Ann Kaplan, "Is the Gaze Male?," in *Feminism and Film*, ed. Ann Kaplan (Oxford: Oxford University Press, 2000), 230.

16 Virginia Woolf, *A Room of One's Own* (New York: Mariner Books, 1989).

17 On Lacan's musings on the matter, see Jacques Lacan, *The Seminar of Jacques Lacan, Book XX (1972-1973): On Feminine Sexuality, the Limits of Love and Knowledge*, trans. Bruce Fink (New York: Norton, 1999). This was also a major theme in de Beauvoir's *The Second Sex*.

18 Kaplan, "Is the Gaze Male?," 124.

19 Laura Mulvey, "Visual Pleasure and Narrative Cinema," in *Feminist Film Theory: A Reader*, ed. Sue Thornham

(New York: New York University Press, 1999), 158. Mulvey's essay was originally published in *Screen* 16, no. 3 (1975): 6–18.

20 Even though Mulvey draws on Lacan in her analysis of the male gaze, the concept should not be confused with how Lacan himself defines "the gaze." I explain the distinction later in the text.

21 Mulvey, "Visual Pleasure and Narrative Cinema," 162–63.

22 Kaplan, "Is the Gaze Male?," 124.

23 Karen Hollinger, "'The Look,' Narrativity, and the Female Spectator in *Vertigo*," *Journal of Film and Video* 39, no. 4 (1989): 18–27, 24.

24 de Lauretis, "Oedipus Interruptus," 89–90.

25 See bell hooks, "The Oppositional Gaze: Black Female Spectators," in *From Reel to Real: Race, Sex, and Class at the Movies* (London: Routledge, 2008). The essay was originally published in hooks's *Black Looks: Race and Representation* (Boston: South End Press, 1992).

26 Ibid., 268.

27 Joan Copjec, *Read My Desire: Lacan against the Historicists* (Cambridge: MIT Press, 1994).

28 This journal published many of the most prominent psychoanalytic film critics, including feminist film critics, of the 1980s. Copjec presents a groundbreaking critique of some of the foundational assumptions of this group of critics in "The Orthopsychic Subject," *October* 49 (1989): 53–71. McGowan presents an overview of the dispute on pages 63–67 of *Psychoanalytic Film Theory and The Rules of the Game* (New York: Bloomsbury Press, 2015).

29 McGowan, *Psychoanalytic Film Theory*, 65.

30 Ibid., 71.

31 Ibid., 72.

32 Lacan gave annual seminars that were transcribed. Many of these were later published as books. The anecdote that follows is from *The Seminar of Jacques Lacan, Book XI: The Four Fundamental Concepts of Psychoanalysis (1964)*, trans. Alan Sheridan (New York: Norton, 1978).

33 Ibid., 95.

34 McGowan, *Psychoanalytic Film Theory*, 74.

35 Slavoj Žižek, *The Fright of Real Tears: Krzystof Kieslowski* (London: British Film Institute, 2001), 34.

36 Ibid., 35.

37 Quoted in Žižek, *The Fright of Real Tears*, 34.

38 In this context, I want to note that McGowan argues that the account of suture that I've extracted from Silverman and relied on throughout my analysis arises from a misreading of Jacques-Alain Miller's original formulation of the concept in "La Suture (Éléments de la logic du signifiant)," *CpA* 1, no. 3 (1966): 37–49. This misreading doesn't originate with Silverman but goes back to earlier critics, such as Jean-Pierre Oudart, Daniel Dayan, and Christian Metz. McGowan's commentary on Miller, and on some of the misreadings of Miller (though not Silverman specifically) can be found on pages 56–63 of *Psychoanalytic Film Theory*. The gist of the disagreement is that, for McGowan, suture has to do with "the incompleteness of the signifying system" (62) rather than with the quest for wholeness that I've emphasized in this book. I've reproduced Silverman's version of the argument because it remains dominant in feminist film theory. Žižek's interpretation (in *The Fright of Real Tears* at least) seems to fall somewhere between the interpretations of Silverman and McGowan. An English translation of Miller's essay by Jacqueline Rose can be found in *Screen* 18, no. 4 (1977–78): 24–34.

39 Žižek, *The Fright of Real Tears*, 32–33.

40 Ibid., 34.

41 Ibid., 33.

42 Ibid., 34–35.

43 Ibid., 35.

44 McGowan, *Psychoanalytic Film Theory*, 64.

45 de Lauretis, "Oedipus Interruptus," 84.

46 I'm referring to Jacques Derrida's notorious account of finding himself under the observing gaze of his cat in *The Animal That Therefore I Am* (New York: Fordham University Press, 2008).

47 Frantz Fanon, *Black Skin, White Masks* (New York: Grove Press, 2008). This text was originally published in 1952.

48 Mulvey, "Visual Pleasure and Narrative Cinema," 64.

49 Ibid.

50 Sigmund Freud, "Fetishism (1927)," in *The Complete Psychological Works of Sigmund Freud*, trans. James Strachey, vol. XXI (London: Hogarth Press, 1961), 147–57.

51 Mulvey, "Visual Pleasure and Narrative Cinema," 65.

52 Joan Riviere, "Womanliness as a Masquerade," in *Psychoanalysis and Female Sexuality*, ed. Hendrik Ruitenbeek (New Haven: College and University Press, 1966), 213. Riviere's essay was originally published in *International Journal of Psychoanalysis* 10 (1929): 3–13.

53 Ibid., 213.

54 Mary Ann Doane, "Film and the Masquerade of Femininity: Theorizing the Female Spectator," in *Feminist Film Theory: A Reader*, ed. Sue Thornham (New York: New York University Press, 1999), 138. Doane's essay was originally published in *Screen* 23, no. 3/4 (1982): 74–87.

55 Judith Butler, *Gender Trouble: Feminism and the Subversion of Identity* (New York: Routledge, 1990).

56 See Michel Foucault, *The History of Sexuality, Volume 1: An Introduction*, trans. Robert Hurley (New York: Vintage, 1980).

57 Michel Foucault, *The Birth of Biopolitics: Lectures at the Collège de France 1978-1979*, trans. Graham Burchell (New York: Picador, 2008).

58 Susan Douglas, *The Rise of Enlightened Sexism: How Pop Culture Took Us from Girl Power to Girls Gone Wild* (New York: St. Martin's Griffin, 2010), 6.

59 Barbara Ehrenreich, *Bright-Sided: How Positive Thinking Is Undermining America* (New York: Picador, 2009).

60 Sara Ahmed, *The Promise of Happiness* (Durham, NC: Duke University Press, 2010).

61 Lauren Berlant, *Cruel Optimism* (Durham, NC: Duke University Press, 2011), 1.

62 Ibid., 170, 174.

63 I reproduce this list from the preface to Mari Ruti, *The Age of Scientific Sexism: How Evolutionary Psychology Promotes Gender Profiling and Fans the Battle of the Sexes* (New York: Bloomsbury Press, 2015).

64 Bobbi Carothers and Harry Reis, "The Tangle of the Sexes," *The New York Times*, April 21, 2013, 9.

65 For a more detailed analysis of the problem, see Mari Ruti, *The Case for Falling in Love: Why We Can't Master the Madness of Love—and Why That's the Best Part* (Naperville, IL: Sourcebooks Casablanca, 2011).

66 Douglas, *The Rise of Enlightened Sexism*, 17, 103.

67 Rosalind Gill and Christina Scharff, "Introduction," in *New Femininities: Postfeminism, Neoliberalism, and Subjectivity*, ed. Rosalind Gill and Christina Scharff (New York: Palgrave Macmillan, 2013), 7.

68 Douglas, *The Rise of Enlightened Sexism*, 103.

69 Hilary Radner, *Neo-Feminist Cinema: Girly Films, Chick Flicks, and Consumer Culture* (New York: Routledge, 2011), 5.

70 Ibid., 196.

71 Ibid., 31.

72 Ibid., 197.

73 Ibid., 10.

74 Douglas, *The Rise of Enlightened Sexism*, 9.

75 Ibid., 13.

76 Yael Sherman, "Neoliberal Femininity in *Miss Congeniality*," in *Feminism at the Movies: Understanding Gender in Contemporary Popular Culture*, ed. Hilary Radner and Rebecca Stringer (New York: Routledge, 2011), 81.

77 Ibid., 90.

78 Ibid., 89.

79 Angela McRobbie, *The Aftermath of Feminism: Gender, Culture, and Social Change* (London: Sage, 2009), 122.

80 Douglas, *The Rise of Enlightened Sexism*, 219.

81 Ibid., 236–37.

82 John Berger, *Ways of Seeing* (London: Penguin Press, 1972), 47.

83 Michelle Lazar, "The Right to Be Beautiful: Postfeminist Identity and Consumer Beauty Advertising," in *New Femininities: Postfeminism, Neoliberalism, and Subjectivity*, ed. Rosalind Gill and Christina Scharff (London: Palgrave Macmillan, 2013), 41.

84 Estella Tincknell, "Scourging the Abject Body: *Ten Years Younger* and Fragmented Femininity under Neoliberalism," in *New Femininities: Postfeminism, Neoliberalism, and Subjectivity*, ed. Rosalind Gill and Christina Scharff (London: Palgrave Macmillan, 2013), 91–92.

85 Ibid., 92.

86 Ibid., 84.

87 Douglas, *The Rise of Enlightened Sexism*, 10.

88 Max Horkheimer and Theodor Adorno, *Dialectic of Enlightenment*, trans. Edmund Jephcott (Stanford: Stanford University Press, 2007). The book was first published in 1944.

89 Elaine Scarry, *On Beauty and Being Just* (Princeton: Princeton University Press, 2001).

90 See my *The Age of Scientific Sexism*.

91 Ariel Levy, *Female Chauvinist Pigs: Women and the Rise of Raunch Culture* (New York: Free Press, 2006), 211.

92 Ibid., 30.

93 Ibid.

94 Ibid.

95 Ibid., 4.

96 Ibid., 94.

97 Ibid., 96.

98 Ibid., 92.

99 Queer critics who have advanced this line of reasoning include Gayle Rubin and Janet Halley. Not coincidentally, the same critics have opted for the kind of queer theory that rejects the contributions of feminism. For an analysis of this conflict, see Sharon Patricia Holland, *The Erotic Life of Racism* (Durham, NC: Duke University Press, 2012).

100 Levy, *Female Chauvinist Pigs*, 91.

101 Ibid., 197.

102 Jessica Ringrose, "Are You Sexy, Flirty, or a Slut? Exploring 'Sexualization' and How Teen Girls Perform/Negotiate Digital Sexual Identity on Social Networking Sites," in *New Femininities: Postfeminism, Neoliberalism, and Subjectivity*, ed. Rosalind Gill and Christina Scharff (London: Palgrave Macmillan, 2013), 122.

103 Rosalind Gill, "Bend It Like Beckham? The Challenges of Reading Gender and Visual Culture," in *Visual Methods in Psychology: Using and Interpreting Images in Qualitative Research*, ed. Paula Reavey (New York: Routledge, 2011), 39.

104 Quoted in Gill, "Bend It Like Beckham?," 39.

105 Douglas, *The Rise of Enlightened Sexism*, 32.

106 Mark Simpson, *Male Impersonators: Men Performing Masculinity* (London: Cassell, 1994), 15.

107 Gill, "Bend It Like Beckham?," 38–39.

Chapter 2

1 Quoted in Ann Chisholm, "Missing Persons and Bodies of Evidence," *Camera Obscura* 15, no. 1 (2000): 123–61, 145.

2 Roger Ebert, *Queue It*, March 23, 1990.

3 Karol Kelley, "A Modern Cinderella," *Journal of American Culture* 17, no. 1 (1994): 1–9, 3.

4 Soyini D. Madison, "*Pretty Woman* through the Triple Lens of Black Feminist Spectatorship," in *From Mouse to Mermaid: The Politics of Film, Gender, and Culture*, ed. Elizabeth Bell, Lynda Haas, and Laura Sells (Bloomington: Indiana University Press, 1995), 225.

5 Claude Smith, "Bodies and Minds for Sale: Prostitution in *Pretty Woman* and *Indecent Proposal*," *Studies in Popular Culture* 19, no. 3 (1997): 91–99, 94.

6 Ibid., 92.

7 Ibid.

8 Ibid., 91, 92. Smith reproduces David Thomson's comparison between Vivian and Audrey Hepburn from "Julia Roberts," *A Biographical Dictionary of Film* (New York: Knopf, 1995), 641.

9 Smith, "Bodies and Minds for Sale," 91, 93.

10 Ibid., 93–94.

11 Ibid., 94.

12 Harvey Roy Greenberg, "Rescrewed: *Pretty Woman*'s Co-opted Feminism," *Journal of Popular Film and Television* 19, no. 1 (1991): 9–13, 12.

13 Ibid., 12–13; emphasis added.

14 Ibid.

15 Ibid.

16 Ibid.

17 Elizabeth Scala, "Pretty Women: The Romance of the Fair Unknown, Feminism, and Contemporary Romantic Comedy," *Film & History* 29, no. 1/2 (1999): 34–45, 35.

18 Greenberg, "Rescrewed," 10–11.

19 Ibid., 11.

20 Ibid., 10–11.

21 Ibid., 9, 11, 13.

22 Madison, "*Pretty Woman* through the Triple Lens of Black Feminist Spectatorship," 226.

23 Ibid., 227.

24 Ibid.

25 Ibid., 229.

26 See Hilary Radner, *Neo-Feminist Cinema: Girly Films, Chick Flicks, and Consumer Culture* (New York: Routledge, 2011).

27 See Radner, *Neo-Feminist Cinema*, on this.

28 Greenberg, "Rescrewed," 11.

29 Radner, *Neo-Feminist Cinema*, 79.

30 Madison, "*Pretty Woman* through the Triple Lens of Black Feminist Spectatorship," 230.

31 Toni Morrison, *Playing in the Dark* (Cambridge: Harvard University Press, 1992), 46.

32 Madison, "*Pretty Woman* through the Triple Lens of Black Feminist Spectatorship," 226.
33 Ibid., 227.
34 See bell hooks, *From Reel to Real: Race, Sex, and Class at the Movies* (New York: Routledge, 2008).
35 Madison, "*Pretty Woman* through the Triple Lens of Black Feminist Spectatorship," 227.
36 Ibid., 232.
37 Chisholm, "Missing Persons and Bodies of Evidence," 146.
38 Ibid., 148.
39 Scala, "Pretty Women," 37.
40 Ibid.
41 Ibid., 38.
42 Ibid.
43 Ibid.
44 Radner, *Neo-Feminist Cinema*, 36, 39.
45 Ibid., 37.
46 Chisholm, "Missing Persons and Bodies of Evidence," 147.
47 Madonne Miner, "No Matter What They Say, It's All About the Money," *Journal of Popular Film and Television* 20, no. 1 (1992): 8–14, 11.
48 Ibid.
49 Ibid., 12.
50 Ibid., 13.
51 Ibid.
52 Jane Caputi, "*Sleeping with the Enemy* as *Pretty Woman*, Part II?," *Journal of Popular Film and Television* 19, no. 1 (1991): 1–8, 6.
53 Ibid., 5.
54 Ibid., 3.
55 Ibid., 7.
56 Sigmund Freud, *Dora: A Case of Hysteria*, trans. Anthea Bell (London: Oxford University Press, 2013).

57 Jane O'Sullivan, "Virtual Metamorphoses: Cosmetic and Cybernetic Revisions of Pygmalion's 'Living Doll,'" *Arethusa* 41 (2008): 133–56, 144.

58 Ibid.

59 Ibid., 147.

60 Ibid.

Conclusion

1 Sara Ahmed, *The Promise of Happiness* (Durham, NC: Duke University Press, 2010), 20.

2 See Alain Badiou, *In Praise of Love*, trans. Peter Bush (New York: The Free Press, 2012).

FURTHER READING

Kaja Silverman, *The Subject of Semiotics* (Oxford: Oxford University Press, 1983). Situated at the intersection of semiotics and psychoanalysis, this book theorizes the concept of suture: the process of luring the viewer into the filmic narrative. Silverman argues that movies produce suture in part because their progression toward narrative resolution promises to heal the spectator's split subjectivity (as theorized by Lacan).

Teresa de Lauretis, *Alice Doesn't: Feminism, Semiotics, Cinema* (Bloomington: Indiana University Press, 1984). Drawing on feminism, semiotics, psychoanalysis, and anthropology, de Lauretis interrogates the ways in which cinema and other cultural discourses, understood as sign systems, construct fictional representations of the notion of "woman."

Constance Penley, *The Future of an Illusion: Film, Feminism, and Psychoanalysis* (Minneapolis: University of Minnesota Press, 1989). In this collection of essays, Penley responds to a series of debates concerning the position of feminism in relation to Hollywood and avant-garde cinema, film theory, academia, pornography, and popular culture. She defends psychoanalytic feminism against the charge of placing too much emphasis on the divided nature of the subject.

Sue Thornham, ed., *Feminist Film Theory: A Reader* (New York: New York University Press, 1999). This anthology gathers together many of the "classics" of early psychoanalytic feminist film theory, such as Laura Mulvey's "Visual Pleasure and Narrative Cinema" and Mary Ann Doane's "Film and the Masquerade: Theorizing the Female Spectator." It covers a wide range of topics, including oppressive images of femininity, "woman" as fetishized object of desire, female spectatorship, and the cinematic pleasures of black women and lesbian women.

E. Ann Kaplan, ed., *Feminism & Film* (Oxford: Oxford University Press, 2000). Covering the final quarter of the twentieth century, this selection of essays traces major developments—theoretical, critical, and practical—on topics related to women and cinema. It provides a detailed analysis of Mulvey's theory of the male gaze.

Yvonne Tasker and Diane Negra, eds, *Interrogating Postfeminism: Gender and the Politics of Popular Culture* (Durham: Duke University Press, 2007). This collection brings feminist perspectives to bear on contemporary mass media, questioning the postfeminist assumption that feminism has accomplished its goals and is now a thing of the past.

Susan Douglas, *The Rise of Enlightened Sexism: How Pop Culture Took Us from Girl Power to Girls Gone Wild* (New York: St. Martin's Griffin, 2010). This book also interrogates the idea that feminism's job is done. Among other things, Douglas takes a critical look at media images of strong women, such as powerful female characters on television shows, arguing that these pop cultural representations mask real and persistent social inequality.

Hilary Radner, *Neo-Feminist Cinema: Girly Films, Chick Flicks and Consumer Culture* (New York: Routledge, 2011). This book shows how the needs of conglomerate Hollywood have encouraged an emphasis on consumer culture within films aimed at women. Radner argues that *Pretty Woman* and other so-called "girly films" advocate neoliberal values, such as a go-getter attitude that relies on the notion that exertion will automatically be rewarded.

Hilary Radner and Rebecca Stringer, eds, *Feminism at the Movies: Understanding Gender in Contemporary Popular Cinema* (New York: Routledge, 2011). Covering a range of genres and issues, this collection examines the ways that contemporary movies reflect changing gender roles. Topics include the gendered political economy of cinema, consumer culture, depictions of professional women, and the intersections of gender, race, and ethnicity.

Melanie Waters, ed., *Women on Screen: Feminism and Femininity in Visual Culture* (Basingstoke: Palgrave Macmillan, 2011). The essays in this collection interrogate how and why certain configurations of embodied female identity persist and are valorized in contemporary cinema and television, engaging in debates regarding the legacies of second-wave feminism and postfeminism.

INDEX

Note: Locators followed by 'n' indicate notes section.

Absent One   48–9
Adam's Rib (1949)   5
Adorno, Theodor   91
Ahmed, Sara   72–3
Alexander, Jason   101
Alias (TV series)   1
Alice Doesn't: Feminism, Semiotics, Cinema (de Lauretis)   31
American Gigolo (1980)   99
Anderson, Pamela   72
Armani ad   96–7, 99
Austen, Jane   4

Banks, Tyra   72
Bauer, Jack   30
Beckham, David   96–9
Beckham, Victoria   97
Bellamy, Ralph   102
Benson, Sheila   106
Berger, John   88
Berlant, Lauren   73
Beyoncé   7, 13, 125
biopolitics   68
Bobbitt, Lorena   165–6
The Bodyguard (1992)   125
The Bride Came C.O.D. (1941)   5
Bridesmaids (2011)   2–3
Bright-Sided (Ehrenreich)   72
Bringing Up Baby (1938)   5

Bullock, Sandra   12, 176
Butler, Judith   63–5, 143

capitalism   114, 118, 139, 161
  consumer   65, 108, 167
  corporate   114
  and heteropatriarchy   113
  neoliberal   10–11, 14, 19, 67–72, 80–2, 87, 179
Caputi, Jane   163–4
castration   22–7, 29, 33, 53, 57–9, 165, 172
character makeover/transformation   146–50
Chicagoreader.com   106
Chisholm, Ann   145–6
Christian Science Monitor   106
Cinderella Story (2004) A   141–2
cinematic suture   29–32, 48–9, 57
"cis-man"/"cis-woman"   7, 184 n.13
codes, gender   33, 55, 63–5, 77, 86, 129, 138
commercialism   68, 173
conspicuous consumption   150–4, 177
consumer capitalism   65, 108, 167

consumerism   10–11, 14, 90, 100, 152, 173, 179
    and heteropatriarchy   87
    and neoliberal capitalism   81
contemporary film criticism   55
Cooper, Bradley   1
Copjec, Joan   45
Coppola, Sofia   143
corporate capitalism   114
Costner, Kevin   125
Craig, Daniel   111
Crawford, Joan   5
criticism   105
    contemporary film   55
    feminist film   18–19
    feminist literary   17
    feminist media   18
    on Pretty Woman (1990)   106–11
    social   107
cruel optimism   73
Cruise, Tom   111
Cumming, Alan   54

Davis, Betty   5
de Beauvoir, Simone   25
de Lauretis, Teresa   31–2, 43–4, 53, 57–8
de Saussure, Ferdinand   25
Delgrough, Dennis   106
Derrida, Jacques   54, 187 n.46
desire   15–16, 18–20, 22, 25–7, 36–8, 40–7, 50–1, 73, 82, 85–6, 91, 94, 97–8, 124–5, 150, 158, 167, 169–72, 178
    female object of   12, 32, 37, 40–1, 43, 146

The Devil Wears Prada (2006)   71, 114
Diaz, Cameron   176
Disney   104, 106, 112
Doane, Mary Ann   62–3
Douglas, Susan   14, 71, 80–3, 86, 88, 90, 98, 152, 178
Downton Abbey (TV series)   30

Ebert, Roger   107, 174, 176
Ehrenreich, Barbara   72
Elizondo, Hector   102, 107
embedded feminism   14, 83, 100, 113
enlightened sexism   83
Entertainment Weekly   106
Ephron, Nora   30
Erin Brockovich (2000)   176
eroticism   12, 22, 37, 41, 58, 86, 110

Fanon, Frantz   54
Female Chauvinist Pigs (Levy)   92
female empowerment   12, 19, 38, 71, 86–7, 93, 96–7, 112–13, 141
female gaze   38, 58
female object of desire   12, 32, 37, 40–1, 43, 146
female sexuality   20, 34–5, 90, 92, 94, 108–9, 137, 169
female spectators   5, 13–14, 39–40, 43–5, 112, 133, 146, 170–1, 175
femininity. *See also Pretty Woman* (1990)
    Freud's psychoanalysis on   20–5, 28–9, 36, 38, 56, 59–60, 76, 165–6

and girliness 79–83, 87
and happiness scripts 72–4
as heteropatriarchy
  32–6, 105
hyperfemininity 19, 65,
  67–8, 80, 177
hypersexualized 9, 34, 81,
  83, 91, 94
Lacanian psychoanalysis
  on 25–30, 32, 45–55,
  57, 59–60, 64, 75,
  90, 165
and lack 24–9, 45, 49,
  57–9, 61–2, 70, 72, 74,
  77, 86, 90–1, 165–7, 172
and male gaze 36–45
masquerade of 13, 55–63,
  65, 85, 87, 100, 115,
  141–7, 158–9, 167–9,
  172–8
and media culture 9, 14,
  17–19, 37, 55–6, 67–8,
  71–2, 79, 85–6, 90–2,
  96–7, 172
neoliberal 84, 86–8,
  90–1, 130, 141, 158,
  170, 173
normative 23, 32, 34, 62,
  65, 67, 77, 85–6, 88,
  145, 175
power femininity 83–6
and sexual self-
  objectification 12, 19,
  67, 83–4, 90–6
turning female subject into
  object 45–54
feminism
  description 6–10
  embedded 14, 83, 100, 113
  fourth-wave 9

postfeminism 10–11, 14,
  19, 70–1, 81–3, 88, 90,
  92, 113
second-wave 6, 11, 17,
  66–7, 80–1, 84, 94, 100,
  113, 172
third-wave 8–9, 44, 62–8,
  81–2, 95, 136, 138–9,
  158, 178
Feminism and Film
  (Kaplan) 34
feminist analysis
  of cinematic suture 29–32,
  48–9
  of Pretty Woman
  (1990) 111–15
feminist film criticism 18–19
feminist literary criticism 17
feminist media 14, 18–19, 37,
  68, 79, 90
fetishism 55–62, 164–8
Forsaking All Others (1934) 5
Foucault, Michel 50, 64,
  68, 87
fourth-wave feminism 9
free-floating gaze 49
French poststructuralism 18
Freud, Sigmund 20–5, 28–9,
  36, 38, 56, 59–60, 76,
  165–6
From Reverence to Rape
  (1974) 18
Frozen (2014) 104–5

Galatea 105, 124, 140
Garner, Jennifer 1
gaze 46–54, 186 n.20
  female 38, 58
  free-floating 49
  male (*See* male gaze)

oppositional 45
surveillance 86–90
white 54
gender
　codes of 33, 55, 63–5, 77, 86, 129, 138
　complementarity 27–8
　differences 77, 79, 133, 178
　inequality 8, 34, 71, 110, 113
　roles 27, 80, 114–15, 134, 138, 178
　and sexuality 6, 15–16, 19, 33, 64, 66
　socialization 33–4, 44, 68
　stereotypes 31, 74–9, 132–8
gendered behavior 34, 63
genderqueer 7, 179, 184 n.13
Gender Trouble (1990) 63
Gere, Richard 1, 99, 101, 107, 111–12
Giacomo, Laura San 101, 107
Gill, Rosalind 81, 97–8
girliness, and femininity 79–83, 87
Girls Gone Wild (videos) 92
Gleiberman, Owen 106
The Good Wife (TV series) 30–1, 54
Gossip Girl (TV series) 87, 121
Grant, Gary 5
Great Divide 138
Greenberg, Harvey Roy 110–12, 122, 126, 129, 131, 155, 162–3

The Hangover (2009) 3
happiness scripts, and femininity 72–4

Haskell, Molly 17–18
Hathaway, Anne 176
Hepburn, Audrey 109
Hepburn, Katharine 5
heroine humanization 173–6
heteropatriarchy 9, 27–8, 34, 36–7, 39, 41–3, 51, 59, 65, 67, 77, 82–3, 88, 90, 92, 95, 98, 177–8
　and capitalism 113
　and consumerism 87
　femininity as 32–6, 105
heterosexuality 22, 34, 94, 98
Hilton, Paris 92–3
His Girl Friday (1940) 5
Hitchcock, Alfred 39, 41–3, 48–51, 55, 57, 105
Hollinger, Karen 43
Homeland (TV series) 30
homo economicus 68
homosexuality 22
hooks, bell 44–5
Horkheimer, Max 91
Houston, Whitney 125
Howe, Desson 106, 114
human sexuality 21–2
hyperfemininity 19, 65, 67–8, 80, 177
hypersexualized femininity 9, 34, 81, 83, 91, 94

Icon of Femininity 35
Internal Affairs (1990) 99
Ipex bra 83

Jenner, Bruce. *See* Jenner, Caitlyn
Jenner, Caitlyn 33
Johansson, Scarlett 143
Jolie, Angelina 35

Kaplan, Ann   34, 36–7
Kelley, Karol   108–9
Kendrick, Anna   176
Kermore, Frank   3
Kutcher, Ashton   127

La Traviata (Verdi)   102, 130
LA Weekly   106
Lacan, Jacques   25–30, 32, 45–55, 57, 59–60, 64, 75, 90, 165
lack, and femininity   24–9, 45, 49, 57–9, 61–2, 70, 72, 74, 77, 86, 90–1, 165–7, 172
Lawton, J. F.   107
Lazar, Michelle   89
Legally Blonde (2001)   71, 114
Levi-Strauss, Claude   25
Levy, Ariel   92–5
loophole woman   93
Lopez, Jennifer   12
L'Oreal   173
Los Angeles Times   106
Lost in Translation (2011)   143

Madison, D. Soyini   108–9, 112, 117, 124–6, 128
Maid in Manhattan (2002)   12, 114
male gaze   12, 50–3, 55–8, 85, 88–9, 91, 100, 115, 143
  and feminity   36–41
  and fetishism   55–62, 164–8
  and *Pretty Woman* (1990)   168–73
  and *Vertigo* (1958)   41–5
  and voyeurism   55–62, 164–5
male psyche   60, 77
male spectator   57

Manolo Blahniks   83
Marshall, Garry   1, 30, 105–7, 112
masculine peacocking   29
masculinity   7, 13, 23–4, 29, 33–6, 44, 61, 63, 65, 66, 77, 90, 136, 138, 140, 145. *See also* phallus
Maslin, Janet   106–7
masquerade, of femininity   13, 55–63, 65, 85, 87, 100, 115, 141–7, 158–9, 167–9, 172–7
McCarthy, Melissa   3
McDonald, Tamar Jeffers   3
McGowan, Todd   45–7, 49–50, 52–3
McRobbie, Angela   87
media culture, and femininity   9, 14, 17–19, 37, 55–6, 67–8, 71–2, 79, 85–6, 90–2, 96–7, 172
Metamorphoses (Ovid)   105
Meyers, Nancy   30
Michelle, Shelley   107, 145, 167
Miner, Madonne   159–60, 162–3
Miss Congeniality (2000)   12, 85–7, 114, 141, 173–4
Morgenstern, Joe   2
Morrison, Toni   125, 127
movie narrative   13, 32, 56–7, 126, 147, 172, 176
movie screen   29, 46
Mulvey, Laura   36–7, 39–41, 43, 45–6, 50, 52–3, 55–7, 59, 89
My Fair Lady (1964)   105–6
Mystic Pizza (1988)   1

narcissism 80, 98, 167
narcissistic gratification 29, 35, 45–6, 48
narrative resolution 48
nature *versus* nurture 33–4
Negra, Diane 3
Neo-Feminist Cinema (Radner) 80
neofeminism 10–11, 14, 19, 70–1, 81–3, 88, 90, 92, 113
neoliberal femininity 84, 86–8, 90–1, 130, 141, 158, 170, 173
neoliberal ideology 113–14, 120–2
neoliberalism/neoliberal capitalism 10–11, 14, 19, 67–72, 80–2, 87, 179
New York Times 3, 76, 106
Next Top Model (TV show) 72
normative femininity 23, 32, 34, 62, 65, 67, 77, 85–6, 88, 145, 175
Novak, Kim 39

Observer 3
Oedipus complex 22–4, 26, 33, 184–5 n.5
Oedipus Rex (Sophocles) 22
oppositional gaze 45
Orbison, Roy 146
O'Sullivan, Jane 166–8, 174
Ovid 105, 124

Parker, Sarah Jessica 172
"patriarchal unconscious" 36
phallus/phallic power 28–9, 33–5, 45, 58, 60–1, 97, 111, 174. *See also* masculinity
The Philadelphia Story (1940) 5
Pitch Perfect (2012) 71, 114, 141
point-of-view shot 49
postfeminism. *See* neofeminism
postfeminist culture 6, 11–12, 79, 81, 84–5, 90–1, 94–5, 100, 137, 158, 178–9
postfeminist women 8–10, 141
poststructuralist theory 66
power
  conception of 64
  femininity 83–6
Pratt, Benjamin 85
Pretty Little Liars (TV series) 87
Pretty Woman (1990) 1–2, 4. *See also* femininity
  character makeover/transformation 146–50
  and Cinderella motif 105, 108, 118, 124, 129–32, 141, 153–7, 177
  conspicuous consumption 150–4
  contradictions of money 119–24
  criticism on 106–11
  and female Pygmalion 139–41
  feminist analysis of 111–15
  and fetishism 164–8
  and gender stereotypes 132–8
  heroine humanization 173–6
  interpretation of 111–15

and male gaze 41–5, 168–73
and masquerade of
femininity 13, 55–63,
65, 85, 87, 100, 115,
141–7, 158–9, 167–9,
172–7
money as
preoccupation 115–19
and narcissism 167
plot of 101–4
racial politics of class
mobility 124–8
refusing the condo 154–8
shopping spree
sequence 158–64
and social defiance 129–32
Pretty Woman boots 172
Pride and Prejudice (1813) 4
The Princess Diaries
(2001) 141
psychoanalysis, on femininity
Freudian 20–5, 28–9, 36,
38, 56, 59–60, 76, 165–6
Lacanian 25–30, 32,
45–55, 57, 59–60, 64, 75,
90, 165
Pygmalion 105, 124, 140

queer critics 22, 190 n.99
queer theory 15, 63–4

racial politics, of class
mobility 124–8
Radner, Hilary 4–5, 80–2, 84,
86, 123, 159
Read My Desire (Copjec) 45
Reader 106
Ringrose, Jessica 96
The Rise of Enlightened Sexism
(2010) 71

Riviere, Joan 60–2, 142
Roberts, Julia 1, 5, 12, 99,
106–8, 111, 132, 145–6,
163, 167, 176
Rolling Stone 3, 92, 106
romantic comedies
(romcoms) 2–6, 11–12,
14–15, 30, 54–6, 67–8,
71, 73, 79, 80, 83, 91,
100, 105, 107–8, 110–15,
118, 121, 123, 125, 127,
131–2, 136–9, 142, 156,
158, 167, 169, 172–4,
176–81
Rosenbaum, Jonathan 106
Rudolph, Maya 3
Russell, Rosalind 5

sardine can 46, 53
Scala, Elizabeth 110, 149–50,
152, 156
Scarry, Elaine 91
Scharff, Christian 81
scopophilia 56
screen, movie 29, 46
Screen (British journal) 46
screwball comedies 5,
183 n.12
The Second Sex (1949) 25
second-wave feminism 6, 11,
17, 66–7, 80–1, 84, 94,
100, 113, 172
self-objectification, sexual 12,
19, 67, 83–4, 90–6
Seminar XI (Lacan) 47
Sex and the City
(TV series) 87
Sex and the City: The Movie
(2008) 80, 121
sexism, enlightened 83

sexual pleasure 93
sexual self-objectification 12, 19, 67, 83–4, 90–6
sexuality 8, 40, 95–6, 158, 172
　female 20, 34–5, 90, 92, 94, 108–9, 137, 169
　and gender 6, 15–16, 19, 33, 64, 66
　human 21–2
　in romcoms 107–8
She Wouldn't Say Yes (1945) 5
Sheehan, Henry 106
Sherman, Yael 83–6, 130
She's All That (1999) 141
Silverman, Kaja 29, 31–2, 46, 48–9, 57, 90, 167
Simpson, Mark 98
Sleeping with the Enemy (1991) 163–4
Smith, Claude 108–9, 112, 117, 129–31, 155
social change 16, 56, 66, 96, 113
social criticism 107
social defiance 129–32
Sophocles 22
Sterritt, David 106
Steward, Jimmy 39
Stone, Emma 176
street harassment, of women 38
The Subject of Semiotics (1983) 29
surveillance gaze 86–90
suture, cinematic 29–32, 48–9, 57
Swift, Taylor 7
"the symbolic order" 26

Ten Years Younger (TV show) 89
third-wave feminism 8–9, 44, 62–8, 81–2, 95, 136, 138–9, 158, 178
Tincknell, Estella 89
Tracy, Spencer 5
Travers, Peter 3, 106–7
24 (TV series) 30
Two Weeks Notice (2002) 114

The Vampire Diaries (TV series) 30, 96
Vertigo (1958) 39, 41, 43, 55, 57, 59, 105, 141, 148, 167, 175
　and male gaze 41–5
"Visual Pleasure and Narrative Cinema" (essay) 37, 186 n.21
Vogue magazine 36
voyeurism 55–62, 164–5

The Wall Street Journal 2
Warner, Helen 3
Washington Post 106
The Wedding Planner (2001) 114
West Side Story (1961) 118
When Harry Met Sally (1989) 4
white gaze 54
Winston, Harry 172
Witherspoon, Reese 174, 176
"Womanliness as a Masquerade" 60
Woolf, Virginia 35

Žižek, Slavoj 45, 47–50, 53

www.ingramcontent.com/pod-product-compliance
Lightning Source LLC
Chambersburg PA
CBHW071842230426
43671CB00012B/2048